The Way
of the
Seabhean

An Irish Shamanic path

Amantha Murphy
with Orla O'Connell

WOMANCRAFT PUBLISHING

PRAISE FOR
THE WAY OF THE SEABHEAN

The Way of the Seabhean delivers a powerful message for our time: we can find an authentic and viable set of spiritual practices by staying close to home and working with visible and invisible lineage keepers. The wisdom of our ancestors is held in the dreaming of the land, our own dreams, stories, rituals and childhood memories. Amantha Murphy's focus is on the Irish Tradition. She uses the Wheel of the Year and the Tree of Life as her glyphs and introduces the reader to a pantheon of ancient (archetypal) Irish goddesses. We live in a time when counter-cultural appropriation is frowned on, travelling carries a carbon footprint and the pandemic has changed our world overnight. This book is medicine for our time: call on your ancestors and deities to create a viable and personal bundle of life-saving spiritual tools! And thank you Orla O'Connell for organising and presenting the material in such an accessible format!

Imelda Almqvist, international teacher and author of three books including *Natural Born Shamans: A Spiritual Toolkit for Life* and *Medicine of the Imagination: Dwelling in Possibility (An Impassioned Plea for Fearless Imagination)*

Amantha Murphy is a living treasure. It has been a great blessing to partake of sacred ceremony with Amantha both in Ireland and here in the United States, where she has brought her integrity and deep, rich spirit to my inipi purification 'sweatlodge' ceremonies and The School of Sacred Studies. The antiquity of Amantha's shamanic soul holds the wisdom of the ages. Through her written words, the voices of our ancestors speak to us. Within these pages are recorded priceless teachings, remembrances, and a gentle roadmap leading us to the spiritual knowledge of our ancestors.

Denise King Francisco, teacher, author and founder of The Temple Within School of Sacred Studies

Amantha teaches us how to weave our personal-cultural way of being in the world and how to relate to the world's soul by retrieving our ancient original instructions in a new way. Amantha travels into the depths of soul; before there are forms. Then, as the masterful midwife she is, she facilitates the birth of archetypes so that we can transform and shape-shift our reality. This transformation will lead us into a new way of harmony with our Mother Earth and remind us that we are all related as we are children of the same Mother.
Aho! Mi Takuye Oyacin – we are all related.

Dr Eduardo Duran, author and PhD psychologist

Amantha Murphy has created a beautiful tapestry that weaves together the threads of an authentic tradition of the Irish Wise Woman. She has brought into the light many wonderful truths, stories, and practices once hidden from mainstream culture, and teaches ways in which the reader can connect with their ancestors, call upon the Irish goddesses, experience the Wheel of the Year, and work with the elements of Earth, for empowerment, healing, and transformation of both person and planet. Amantha has lived and taught The Way of the Seabhean for many years to those who journeyed to Ireland in search of one as genuine, heart-centred, and wise as herself. Now, through this book, these profound yet very accessible teachings are available to all those looking for genuine Celtic wisdom.

Mara Freeman, author *Kindling the Celtic Spirit* and *Grail Alchemy*

Take the time to relish this book. Curl up by the fire with a nice cup of tea or a glass of poitín, and let yourself remember the wisdom of the Grandmothers. Amantha Murphy as the seabhean and Orla O'Connell as her scribe create an environment of total immersion where the ways of the women are held as sacred. Murphy shares the teachings she received from her grandmother, and while these are specific to Ireland the knowledge also feels universal. I found myself wishing I could have sat at her Granny's feet too. This world so needs all this wisdom right now!

Gina Martin, High Priestess of Triple Spiral of Dún na Sidhe, author *Sisters of the Solstice Moon* and *Walking the Threads of Time* (Books I and II of the *When She Wakes* series)

The Way of the Seabhean offers techniques for exploring the possibility of deep soul healing, through our connection to the land and the seasons, and through our relationship to our ancestors and the sacred. This book weaves together a modern tradition with an ancient flavour and resonance.

Eimear Burke, Chosen Chief of the Order of Bards, Ovate and Druids

A heartwarming introduction to the wise woman's way in the Irish Celtic tradition. The personal stories, both handed down and intuited, add genuine soul to the journey with the sacred feminine, via the Wheel of the Year, encouraging accessibility to the teachings.

Heidi Wyldewood (Barefoot Heartsong), healer, teacher, mentor, priestess, ceremonialist and sacred activist

This is an important and timely book. It gathers essential wisdom from our ancient traditions, wisdom crucial for us humans to embrace at this time. Amantha has crafted a deep resource book which has the capacity to awaken within the reader an awareness of the riches of our past spiritual traditions. This book is influenced by her deep relationship as a child with her maternal grandmother in Kerry and with her life journey and studies over many years. She describes the appropriate ways that these gifts can be used to support and resource us to deal effectively with the challenges present in our current society. She stresses the importance of story as a way of reconnecting with the deep wisdom held within our traditions and emphasises that the recovery of these ancient threads will support each of us to be a part of weaving the fabric of a new and sustainable society.

Dolores T. Whelan, author of *Ever Ancient Ever New: Celtic Spirituality in the 21st century*, spiritual guide and teacher within the traditions of this land

Teaching within the Celtic traditions myself, I was already following Amantha Murphy as a sister-priestess, but mostly in spoken form or online. Therefore, finding her new book The Way of the Seabhean felt a significant synchronicity. Working in these traditions, we often reclaim the old ways, and Amantha does this beautifully and firmly grounded in her own Irish-Celtic heritage and Irish Shamanic tradition. By bringing in the new title of the Seabhean, Amantha offers a powerful introduction in how to walk this ancient pathway into our modern times. Through these very comprehensible teachings, she offers old and new ways of interconnectedness with Mother Earth, which is definitely what we all need in these times!

Marion Brigantia van Eupen, co-organiser of The Goddess Conference, tutor of the Brighde-Brigantia trainings

Published by Womancraft Publishing, 2020
womancraftpublishing.com

ISBN 978-1-910559-63-5
Also available in ebook format: ISBN 978-1-910559-62-8

Cover art: Angie Latham, celticmystery.co.uk
Cover design and typesetting: Patrick Treacy, lucentword.com
'The Way of the Seabhean' © Amantha Murphy
Aerial photograph of Ireland © NASA Earth Observatory
Tree of Life © Philippa Gossage
Chakra image © JoAnn Turner

Womancraft Publishing is committed to sharing powerful new women's voices, through a collaborative publishing process. We are proud to midwife this work, however the story, the experiences and the words are the author's alone. A percentage of Womancraft Publishing profits are invested back into the environment reforesting the tropics (via TreeSisters) and forward into the community.

To my four children, my greatest acts of creation,
and to all who come after me.

OTHER BOOKS BY THE AUTHORS

Drinking from the Source, Amantha Murphy
The Man with No Skin, Órfhlaith Ní Chonaill (Orla O'Connell)

CONTENTS

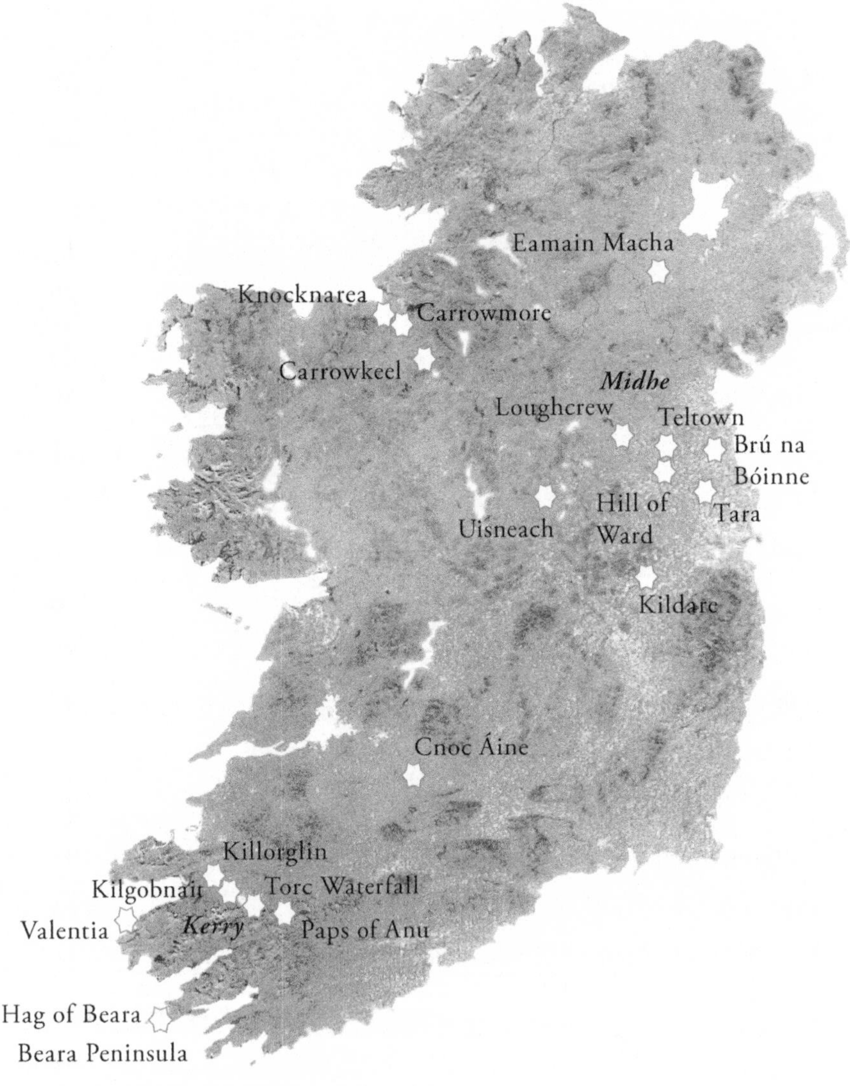

Eamain Macha

Knocknarea
Carrowmore

Carrowkeel

Midhe

Loughcrew
Teltown

Brú na
Bóinne

Hill of
Ward

Uisneach

Tara

Kildare

Cnoc Áine

Killorglin

Kilgobnait
Torc Waterfall

Valentia
Kerry

Paps of Anu

Hag of Beara
Beara Peninsula

Map of Ireland showing places of relevance.

*The world is a weave of energy
and every human being is
a thread on that Great Weave.*

*Each one of us also creates
our own, unique weave
which vibrates around us.
This energetic weave attracts
everything we need in life.*

ACKNOWLEDGEMENTS

Ϝɪʀꜱᴛ, ɪ ᴡᴏᴜʟᴅ ʟɪᴋᴇ ᴛᴏ ᴀᴄᴋɴᴏᴡʟᴇᴅɢᴇ
my ancestors, my grandmother, my parents and my spirit guides for always being there with me throughout my life. I acknowledge my 'sister' Margaret for being the balance and the powerhouse and for all the work she did over the years, for the care and the holding of space. I need to acknowledge my ex-husband, for helping me to take on all that I am and for pushing me to do that. I acknowledge and thank my four amazing and creative adult children for the teachings they have brought to me, as much as for the love, fulfilment and heart space I share with them. I would like to acknowledge and thank the apprentices, each and every one, for drawing the teachings through me. I would like to acknowledge and thank Margot for her love and support over twenty years – we learnt so much together. And I acknowledge and bow down to Orla, for her marathon work in getting this book from a dream into a reality.

FOREWORD

My friend Amantha Murphy is a seabhean – a female shaman, healer and visionary. The tradition of the seabhean has been passed down through generations of Irish women from ancient times, possibly since the time of the Tuatha Dé Danann. The Irish word *seabhean* (pronounced 'sha-van') comes from County Donegal.

Amantha's gifts came from her Kerry grandmother, who was a healer and midwife. Throughout our history, these women have been highly respected in their communities, but were often persecuted by the Catholic Church and the authorities. Because of this, their presence and practices have been kept secret.

Amantha has taken the courageous and generous path of bringing her gifts out into the world and sharing them with others. She teaches the Way of the Seabhean through workshops and has initiated many women in the Irish shamanic ways, through her apprentice trainings. She believes, and has proved, that these practices and this way of being in the world are not confined to the few who inherit it, but can be learnt and used by all of us to grow to our full potential as human beings. Her workshops and apprenticeships have brought healing and personal growth to many women and some men, not only in Ireland but in the USA and Canada.

I had known Amantha for years and had attended some of her inspirational and joyful workshops at the Wise Woman Weekend. As dyslexia prevented her from writing this book herself, she approached me to scribe it for her. I hesitated at first as I was busy writing a novel. That afternoon, I attended a workshop in which she kept thirty women spellbound for an hour and a half. I thought to myself, if this is not written down, the world will be poorer.

Six months later, on Brigid's Day, my journey with the seabhean began. I was given more than two hundred recordings of workshops and apprentice trainings and Amantha's vision, which was the image of a woman, a tree and a chalice. It was a huge task that took over my life, to the exclusion of everything else, for four-and-a-half fascinating years.

First, I had to listen to all of those recordings (some of which were five hours long), map out what was where in which recording and type up relevant material. As these had been recorded with different groups over a number of years, there was a lot of repetition, but also very different versions of the various elements and each piece was in its own specific context, rather than in a form suitable for this book. I often thought, over the years, that it would be much easier to sit Amantha down and get her to dictate the whole book. But, doing it that way, a lot of rich material would have been lost.

Amantha is a born storyteller and, in her teaching, she weaves a wonderful web of story, anecdote, wisdom and practical advice, all enriched with the oral tradition that she has inherited. All these threads needed to be unpicked and rewoven again into an accessible and readable book. And I could not fill in the gaps in my own words – I had to trawl through recordings and transcripts to find the exact phrase or paragraph that I needed. I also worked with Amantha in person, or remotely, to fill in bigger gaps. Every word of this book is Amantha's – only the glossary and footnotes are my additions.

This book combines the hidden lore of wise women with insights gathered in Amantha's own journeying. It still reflects Amantha's initial image – the woman, the tree and the chalice. The first section (the woman) introduces us to the world of the seabhean, her roles and practices. It gives insights into Amantha's life and her bond with the grandmother who taught her.

The second part presents the Tree of Life, symbolising the three worlds: Lower World, the ancestors (roots of the tree), Middle World, the reality in which we live (trunk of the tree), and Upper World, the spiritual world (branches of the tree).

*The three elements of the Seabhean: the woman, the tree of
life and the chalice. Painting by Philippa Gossage.*

These are the realms where the seabhean journeys to bring back
what is needed for healing and for balancing energies. Journeying
is a theme throughout the book and Amantha has provided links to
recordings of some journeys to enable the reader to experience this
for themselves for their own healing and balance.

In the Lower World section, we journey and work with our guides
to find and heal ancestral patterns that may be holding us back in
life. We learn to embrace our instinctive, animal nature, so that we
can become whole.

The Wheel of the Year is an ancient calendar, containing seasonal
turning points such as Samhain (Hallowe'en) and Imbolc (Brigid's
Day). Here it is used as a powerful tool. Each of the eight points

of the Wheel has an Irish goddess associated with it. As well as the better-known goddesses, Medb and Brigit, we meet Tailtiú, Boann, Macha, Tlachtga, Áine and the Cailleach. These goddesses are archetypes, aspects of ourselves, which can help us to understand and embrace our many facets as human beings, for instance, passion with Medb and the hidden, unacceptable, parts of ourselves that we hide with Macha in the cave of our becoming and undoing. There is also a wealth of folklore in the traditions of the wheel and there are Amantha's personal journeys with the goddesses.

Women's blood has always been thought to have magical powers. The chalice symbolises the womb. The third part of the book is the chalice and the priestessing role of women, which means recognising people, things and situations and bringing them into the sacred.

The chapter on rituals and rites of passage reflects Amantha's passion for this subject. She says, "When we honour those transitional times and experiences in our lives, we come home to the soul, recognising our spiral journey as one of unfolding and beauty." She is a spiritual celebrant, through the Spiritual Union of Ireland and legally performs marriages and handfastings. I have had the pleasure of participating in some deeply moving and, at the same time, playful opening and closing ceremonies that she organised for the Wise Woman Weekend.

In the process of scribing this book, I became passionate about the Way of the Seabhean. It changed me. I gained insights, practices and skills that enhanced my own life. I learnt to detach myself emotionally from situations, so that I could be less involved but more supportive of the people I love.

At the centre of this work is a deep connection with the earth and a belief that we are meant to be here now, for our unique soul's purpose and for the benefit of the earth. This book helps us to recognise our essential relationship with our earth and all the people and creatures who live on it. It reminds us of the interdependency of all living things. The seabhean path also takes us beyond this reality, opening us to unseen realms within and around us. There is space for magic, fairies and even leprechauns!

Some parts of this tradition were familiar to me from my own childhood in Kerry. Our local, friendly farmer was steeped in fairy lore and I remember the traditions of Brigid's crosses, the Biddies and the blessing of wells. It is a wonder to see all of this, which is part of the ether in Kerry, put in context and written down (much of it for the first time). And it has been my privilege to scribe it, not just for Amantha, but for myself and for everyone who is curious or who is seeking to reconnect with themselves or with the ways of our ancestors.

Amantha uses the word 'shamanic' to describe the way in which the seabhean operates. While this work is essentially Irish, it also belongs to a worldwide shamanic system. And while it is a personal journey, it is relevant to anyone seeking meaning, healing and connection in their lives.

Orla O'Connell M.Phil (Creative Writing)

Author of the prizewinning novel, *The Man with No Skin*.
Strandhill, County Sligo
July 30, 2020

THE SEABHEAN

Tⱶe seⱥꝺheⱥꝺ (pronounced 'sha-van')
is the Irish female shaman, healer and seer, the woman who walks
between the worlds. She is able to move betwixt and between realities
to bring back information that is needed for her people. The seabhean
is held in high regard in her community. This role has passed down
through the female line in families since ancient times.

The seabhean is the woman who holds the presence of the weave
of life and is conscious of the roles of all people, of nature and of the
planet and our intricate role within that. She does not interfere or
seek to control but to bring balance, assisting in balancing the weave
on a personal level with people and on an earth level with nature and
with our Great Mother. On a planetary level, she assists with our role
in balancing the Great Weave of our multiverse.

These women have existed throughout time, often unrecognised
and unknown by others. They are not particular to Ireland. Although
I am talking about our tradition here, these women were, and are,
all over the world. Some know what they are doing; others are not
necessarily aware of what they carry and how they touch gently into
the weave with other people. They do not seek personal recognition;
their work is for the benefit of their communities and the world.

Traditionally, every tribe had a woman elder who could minister
to those who were ill, have visions, perform soul retrieval, help souls
to pass on, assist children to be born, remember the stories of the
tribe and remind the women of who they were through the stories.
She was able to hold sacred space and create ceremonies. The woman
elder was the healer, midwife, mediator, seer and initiator. She was
also the keeper of the fire.

Over the centuries, the shamanic practices of the seabhean have been misunderstood and misinterpreted. Across the world, hundreds of thousands of women were killed in witch hunts. Many of these women were healers, midwives and herbalists. Some were women who had power or positions, or who wanted to sell land. This violence against women caused a great closing, a great silence. Women's voices and women themselves were closed down. The ancient women's practices became hidden and secret.

From my work with apprentice groups over the years, I have found that the skills of the seabhean may be shared and evoked in other women. The seabhean is you; the seabhean is me. With training, practice and with remembering, we can all embrace our inner seabhean.

My Tradition

In this book, I share my teachings with you. Some of them are universal, others are unique to me. My teachings are not necessarily yours. I share them with you to assist you in finding your own teachings within them, or to awaken your teachings in you.

When I speak about my tradition, I mean the tradition that lies within my blood and my bones. My teachers are my granny, my ancestors, Spirit, the living earth, the Great Mother, the Tuath Dé, the Stone People*, the tree brethren, my animal helpers, the fairies and elementals. They have all sustained me in my life and have shared parts of this tradition with me. Now I claim this as my tradition. It is not only mine; it belongs to all those who consciously carry the bloodline of those who walked before them.

As a child, listening to stories of the Tuatha Dé Danann, Sionann and Medb†, I began the journey of accessing my tradition. I was able to enter into those stories and draw from them parts of who I was. I

* See chapter on Middle World Tools.

† For guidance on pronunciation and background to historical figures and places you may be unfamiliar with, please refer to the Glossary and Pronunciation Guide at the back of the book.

began to reclaim memories. In the beginning I did not know whether I was picking up memories from other lives that I might have lived, or if I was accessing the ancient knowledge that I carried from my forebears in my own DNA. After a while, it did not matter which it was. Those traditional teachings and ancestral memories, together, have informed my work.

The stories are an integral part of our tradition, reminding us of what is in our DNA – awakening those memories in us. Once awakened, they can begin to integrate into our lives and consciousness. The stories feed us.

I share some of these stories along with my teachings of the Way of the Seabhean, so that everybody can find their place within this tradition and can activate or cultivate the gifts that they have, allowing the seabhean to operate within and through them.

My Story

My parents moved to England before I was born, because there was no work available in Ireland at that time. We lived in an area of London called West Kilburn. Some people called it County Kilburn, because so many Irish people lived there. As an emigrant, you are more Irish than the Irish at home, because of the pain. My father never got over leaving Ireland. Every year, when we came back, he cried because he was happy to go home. Then, he cried returning to England, because he had to leave again. My father was fond of a few pints. Like a lot of emigrants, he drank as a way of overcoming that pain of disconnection.

Many Irish were very poor in England after the war. We lived and slept in one room and there was an outside toilet, which we shared with everybody else in the house. Living in such a contained space made me retreat further into my own world.

My brother and I spent our childhood summers in Ireland with my grandmother. She lived where I live now, in County Kerry, on land that belonged to her and to her mother's people. Granny was a beautiful woman who valued and respected the earth. Often, she took us out to talk to the fairies[*] and we left gifts of sugar sandwiches for them. When she made a loaf of bread, she always broke the first piece off and put it out for the fairies. All the old people in that area were constantly aware of the invisible realms. Granny brought me up with that awareness of the other world.

Granny, Ellen Mary Marshall (née Doody).

The spiritual realm was the actual world for me and the fairies were my friends. Everyday life was something difficult that I had to deal with. I am dyslexic which meant that I could not read or write properly and I still cannot learn from books. Some of the teachers thought my inability to learn was just wilfulness and I was beaten at home because of this. That, too, made me retreat into my own, inner world.

My growing up years in London were spent pretending, trying to be like others, hiding behind others and hoping not to get caught out on what I did not know. Other people and children seemed asleep or unaware in some way that I could not understand or fathom, so I spent most of my spare time on my own.

The only time I felt alive was when I was in Ireland with my grandmother. It was home. My granny was four foot two and had a very slight frame. Only her hands were big. She had white hair in two plaits, which she wore across her head or rolled above each ear.

* Fairies: See chapter on Other Middle World Elements/Elements and Elementals.

Granny was a midwife and healer. Her husband died when she was pregnant with the last of her six children. The loss propelled her into doing midwifery. She had a hard life, caring for her children on her own, but she never complained.

Granny used to say, "If you can't say anything good about someone, don't say anything at all." She also said, "If you can't see anything good in them, that's your limitation."

I am told that she delivered sixty-three children into the world and that she never lost one. After Granny assisted a woman in giving birth, she often lived on their farm until the mother was back on her feet. Sometimes it could be two or three weeks. She milked cows, fed chickens, washed clothes, cooked meals and took care of the children. So she became everybody's granny.

She was loved by the community. They never paid her with money, but took care of her and kept her in kind. She always had vegetables, eggs and milk. Sometimes, when we opened the door, there was a chicken hanging in a bag outside or, if a family killed a pig, they gave her cuts of meat. That is how the people paid her.

Granny was my greatest teacher. As a child I wished to be like her. It was wonderful to see the love that people had for her and the esteem in which she was held. Even then, I was conscious of being blessed to be in her company. I had my own secret world with her, which other people did not share. She showed and told me things and whispered things to me.

Granny balanced her life between her beliefs and her Catholic faith. She was born in the late nineteenth century and her Catholicism was loose and easy, retaining elements of pre-Christian beliefs. If she could not get to Mass on Sunday, she said, "Ah sure, God knows I'm busy." She often said to us, "Ah sure, you don't want to pray to Jesus. No, you pray to the Mother. And if you want anything, it's her that will get it for you." There was always a picture of the sacred heart of Mary with a blue light under it, at the bottom of the stairs.

In the Catholic tradition in the south of Ireland, there was a strong devotion to Mary, to the Mother. Near where Granny lived, there are two mountains called The Paps of Anu. They look like breasts, really good triple D cups. There is no mistaking what they are! Ancient people built cairns, like nipples, one on top of each mountain. The Paps has been a place of continued worship of the Great Mother for over four thousand years and the energy of the Great Mother is still strong in the South. That was what I grew up with and She was my deity.

For me the land in Ireland was my mother. She talked to me as I lay on the grass. Where my granny lived, where I live now, is on a high hill looking down into the valley and up into the mountains. When I went home every year, I fell into that field and lay in the grass, spread out like a star, my legs and arms opened out on either side of me. I waited until I became that field and then the hill and the valley, going up into the mountains. My chest opened up and I felt that I could breathe again. She came then and talked to me. I always called her 'She' or 'Her', this ancient woman energy that I knew was my mother.

I felt a little guilty about my own mother, who was a good woman whose whole life focused around taking care of her children and making life good for them. Yet, this energy in the land was my real mother.

Granny saw them in and saw them out. If someone was sick or dying, people sent for her. Often, she knew someone was dying because she heard them calling in the night. She could be sitting by the fire and say to us, "Jack Dowd's passing through and I have to go".

When I was sixteen, I had to send a telegram back to Granny, my mother and my aunt in Kerry, telling them that my uncle (Granny's son and their brother) had died in England. Granny had my mum and aunt dressed and ready to go before the postman got there. She had heard the banshee and had spoken to Jimmy when he died.

When I was nineteen or twenty, I met the medium Owen Potts. Before I knew what was happening, I had asked him if I could join a development group for potential mediums. By the time I was twenty-two, through Owen's guidance, I started doing trance work. Trance mediumship is a type of shapeshifting where one sits in an altered state and allows spirit to talk through them, for the person or persons sitting with them.

People came to me for readings and I did not charge them. I said to spirit, "I cannot keep giving readings. I need to get a job to earn money."

Spirit replied, "What is your problem? We've given you the tools."

I realised then that I was supposed to be charging money; there was supposed to be an exchange.

A dear friend sat with me while I did trance work. Spirit talked through me and often called me 'the shaman'. At the time, we did not know what that word meant.

During my twenties and thirties, I married twice in England and had four children. I went home to see Granny when she was dying. Before I left, I said to my second husband, "The only thing I'd like of Granny's is her wedding ring. I'd love to have something that held her energy." It was not her original ring, because that had worn to nothing. My mum had bought her a ring and had it blessed by the friars. Granny wore that and was very proud of it. It held her energy.

When we got to Killarney, I went straight to the hospital. Granny was tiny, like an eight-year-old in the bed. Her hair was silvery white and she had very clear, blue eyes. When I looked into her eyes I was transported, completely gone. Suddenly, I was standing in the presence of a being that was neither male nor female, it was just pure energy. I knew without words that this being had chosen to come back into this life for the needs of humanity. It placed a white lily between my breasts. I could feel my body vibrating.

I do not know how long I was there, seconds, minutes, or half an hour; then this being released me and I came back to myself.

Granny was looking up at me. She pointed to her ring and nodded. My mother was sitting beside the bed and then she realised that I was there. Mum said, "Oh, she's admiring your ring". I said no. Afterwards I told her about the exchange with Granny and my mother gave the ring to me.

In my early thirties, I stayed with the Native American Hopi tribe on their reservation. An old Native American woman asked me why I was there. "You carry the lineage of your people's tradition," she said. "You carry the stories. You shouldn't be here." I knew it was true. It was like another wake up call. That brought me back to my own home, my own stories and my own land.

After that, I began weaving back to Ireland through my work with the land. In 1995, there was a conference in Killarney, organised by a group from California. A woman at the conference asked if I lived locally and if I had seen fairies. "Oh, yes!" was my reply.

Suddenly, a group of women was asking me to take them to my special, sacred spaces. So I asked spirit, "What am I meant to do?"

I heard the words: "Bring them on pilgrimage." So I went back and told them, "I will take you, but we will have to prepare first. You will have to meditate and attune, to be in the right space."

When we had prepared ourselves, I took them out for the day. They absolutely adored it and, to my surprise, so did I. Two of them actually did see fairies. The next day I took another group out on to the land. This began my Pilgrimages to the Sacred Sites in Ireland.

Gradually, I was finding out what the word shamanic meant. I understood that every indigenous culture has its own way of attuning and working with the earth, ancestors, elements and elementals and its own way of connecting with spirit. All of these ways are loosely termed 'shamanism' now. What Granny had taught me was part of that. It was strange, because at home when she shared her knowledge, we did it quietly, privately, talking by the fire or out in the field. Then I met a group of shamans in Phoenix, Arizona. At first, I was shocked that they were so open. Where I came from it was hidden.

The main reason I use the word shamanic is because people know exactly what I am talking about and the realms within which I work. If I used an Irish name they would not. The name I use and claim is the word seabhean. The seabhean is the woman who carries the ancient mysteries. It is an old Irish name. The word *'sea*[*] (pronounced 'sha') in Irish means strength, it also means regard or esteem. *Bean* (pronounced 'ban')[†] means woman. Many of the attributes of the seabhean are contained within the word itself. The work I do is all woven into this.

In 1997, after separating from my second husband, I went back to

---

[*]   'Sea meaning 'yes' is a combination of the words 'is' and 'ea', so the ' is needed because the letter i is missing.

[†]   These two Irish words combine as a compound noun, so the second element has a h added after the b which softens the sound from 'b' to 'v'.

Kerry to spend two weeks there. I was on my own, lying in the field, and She came to me and told me that I could return. "It's time to come home," She said.

Within three months, I moved home with my two youngest children. Kerry is my soul home and I have lived on the ancestral land ever since. Down the hill are my cousins and others who have become family over the years.

Going back to Ireland with two children was hard because, I knew I would be the only one in the house with them and, it would be a huge change after living in community. I realised that I would need to support them and be there for them. That was very important. I put out the intention that when my third child went to university, I would like to travel again. Before I had my last two children, I had been working a lot in Europe, doing workshops and giving readings.

The year my third daughter went to university, I met two women who asked if I would come to Florida to give a talk about Ireland. My daughter went to university in September and I went to Florida in October. That started me travelling again and my Sacred Pilgrimages were growing. It was exactly as it was meant to be.

Since then, my work has continued to grow and flow. I now offer a variety of workshops and continue to organise pilgrimages to sacred sites in Ireland and to share the Irish myths. In recent years, I started apprentice groups where women learn the Way of the Seabhean, the woman's path, so that they can be all that they are meant to be in the wholeness of their nature. I run apprentice groups in Ancient Irish Shamanism for both women and men and I facilitate rituals and rites of passage. Some of this work is in Ireland, some in the USA and Canada. Since 2016, I have become a spiritual celebrant, through the Spiritual Union of Ireland, legally able to perform marriages and handfastings.

We have a saying in Kerry, "the wheel turns". For me, the wheel has turned and turns again on my journey through life. Spirit, the fairies, the Stone People and the land Herself held me as a child. Now I am opening these realms to others and supporting them on their journeys. I walk my path, open to the mother's heartbeat as my drumbeat, recognising that every step I take is a prayer upon our sacred Mother Earth.

The Way of the Seabhean

Many people of Western European descent, having rejected the religion of their childhood, have searched for a deeper spiritual truth and reality. This search has brought them to shamanic traditions from around the world. They have taken on lessons and traditions from many other cultures: from India in the 1960s, North America (Native Americans) in the 1970s and from South America in the early years of the 21st Century. But many of us have Celtic and pre-Celtic roots and shamanic traditions of our own, which have been lost or covered up.

The word 'shamanism' is used to explain spiritual and energetic work that is done "between the worlds", and many traditions go back thousands of years. Although they may never have connected with each other, shamanic cultures tend to have similar belief structures and similar hieroglyphs. For example, the spiral is important to the Aboriginal people in Australia, as it is for the Irish.

Traditionally, every group or clan had its shaman/medicine person. The shaman's training often starts from birth, although they may not know it. That training leads them to the point on the path where they are ready to take on the work that needs to be accomplished or worked through.

Indigenous peoples were, and are, attuned to the one presence, the one energy. They believe in separate realities. These are the three main realms in our tradition: Lower World, Middle World and Upper World. Shamans assist in keeping the balance of nature and of life. They can walk between the worlds and journey for the needs of others. They can also assist a family or individual in releasing ties or patterns that no longer support them. Many can go into a trance state or shapeshift to bring through information that is necessary for the individual, group, or clan. They can see beyond and see within.

While male shamans exist throughout indigenous cultures, my focus here is on the Irish tradition of the female seabhean, which has been passed down to me through the female line. In Ireland we had indigenous peoples whose culture was matrifocal, where men, as well as women, had roles in honouring the feminine goddesses and Mother Earth. When Christianity came, that brought a patriarchal belief system which lived side-by-side with the older traditions for a time. Although the ancient shamanic tradition has been suppressed over the centuries, it has not gone away entirely. It has been kept hidden, but has been passed down orally through the generations, particularly from mother to daughter or grandmother to granddaughter.

When I inherited this tradition it was nameless. After much searching, the word that came up for me, from a woman elder in Donegal, was the word *seabhean*. The word felt right to me. *'Sea!* (yes!) was an exclamation I already used as an affirmation in rituals. The elder told me that, in Donegal, the word seabhean is also used as the old *(sean)* woman *(seanbhean)* or the wise woman.

The Way of the Seabhean is the woman's path into the ancient Irish mysteries. It is a blend of our ancient shamanic teachings and the women's mysteries which include rites of passage and the rituals and ceremonies that hold and sustain us throughout life. It also includes priestessing, which means recognising people, things and situations and bringing them into the sacred.

In reclaiming these mysteries, we bring together a very ancient way of being. Rites of passage go back through time and were part of every indigenous culture in the world. Recognition of the different realms: Lower World (ancestors), Middle World (present reality) and Upper World (place of spirit), is something that has been understood throughout time.

There are some elements in this book which you will recognise as archetypical to shamanic work, while others are personal to my teachings: the Way of the Seabhean.

Rooted in the Land

Granny taught me to connect with the land and that She would bring me everything I needed. She told me that the earth is my mother and, if I needed something, I should ask Her. My grandmother believed that, if you are sick you go and lie on the earth and if you have arthritis you go and garden, put your hands and feet into the earth to draw out the stiffness (as well as rubbing *poitín* – a traditional Irish spirit alcohol – on it).

One of the stories of my childhood was the Story of Our Land, in which Ireland was once a land of trees and stones. The trees communed with each other and could lift up their roots and move slowly from one place to another. They could also talk with the Stone People. This went on for hundreds of thousands of years.

Coming home to Ireland each year, I felt a deep kinship with the living earth, her trees and stones. They were my friends and talked to me, shared with me and showed me things, places and ways of journeying. From childhood, trees have always been important to me. They have held me and whispered to me.

Stones and rocks are the bones of the earth and hold the stories of the land. It was Granny who first taught me to walk anticlockwise around ancient monuments, to access information there. When I attune to them, the stones can share those stories with me. It is sometimes quite uncanny how closely the stories that I access in this way can match the stories told by the local people in that place.

Traditionally in Ireland, the bards were the keepers of the stories of the tribe, reminding the people of who they were. The bard's position was second only to the head chieftain's. According to the old stories, chieftains and bards could be either male or female. Each clan had their own bards and it might take up to thirty-five years for somebody to be fully trained. They studied in what were called bardic or druidic schools and trained to be visionaries, often having clairvoyance or clairaudience. Some worked with herbs. Others could travel between the worlds, making shamanic journeys. They began as *filí*, poets. Some went on to become bards, druids or ovates. The bards were storytellers and musicians. The druids had magic and were often advisers to the chieftains. Ovates could journey between the worlds. This went on for hundreds of years before and during the coming of the Celts.*

When the Celtic culture came to Ireland, it brought customs and lore that became interwoven with the earlier, ancient traditions. I do not try to separate them from each other.

It is said that each Celtic tribe that came would fight the tribes that were already there. Then a new tribe would come in and fight them for the land. That happened over a period of eight hundred years. In that time, it was important that they kept the stories which reminded them of what had happened, of what was right and wrong, of who did well and who was wronged. It was on that lore that the Brehon Laws were based in later times. The Brehon Laws were to do with what was right and with keeping the society in balance.

The first stories were written down in Ireland around AD 400. Many were transcribed by Christian monks who chose and adapted the stories to suit their patriarchal belief system. Despite efforts by the Irish Catholic Church to suppress the oral tradition in the twentieth century, it has continued right up until the present day. The oral tradition is still very strong and contains versions of older stories which reflect the ancient, matrifocal tradition.

Because the bards worked betwixt and between, they were not accepted by Christians. They were gradually moved out from their position, until they became the *seanchaí*, the story tellers. Even up to the 1940s and 1950s, *seanchaí* travelled around Ireland, staying in one place or another. They were respected. People took them into their homes and fed them. As well as sharing the ancient stories, they carried news of people's relatives and what was happening in the next village.

The stories, as they were told to me by Granny and her friends, had been passed down from generation to generation since ancient times, perhaps even since the time of the Tuath Dé themselves. These were part of the Kerry oral tradition and have never been written down.

---

* Although some researchers cast doubt on whether large numbers of Celts came to Ireland, the coming of the Milesians is an integral part of the folklore and landscape in Kerry. When I speak about the Celts, I am drawing my information from the oral tradition.

They bear the marks of the many storytellers who retold them over the centuries. Some incorporate Christian elements and themes (for example, in the version of the *Táin* which was told to me, Cúchulainn had been converted to Christianity).

Our stories lie in our bones. They are a magical part of the weave of our lives. They are a section of the rich tapestry which feeds into us and from which we can draw. The ancient stories of our land, this land, Ireland, weave us in right relationship with all.

For me, this tradition is integral to the fabric of the land I live on and to the fabric of Ireland. You can imagine that fabric like a *brat* (a cloak) that you put around you. It enfolds you, it keeps you warm, it feeds, nourishes, sustains and awakens you. This is the fabric that has given me this tradition.

My work is rooted in the ancient Irish tradition and the shamanic way of working, which my grandmother shared with me. What I know, what I feel, what sustains me, what works is the teachings that come through me. (I use the word 'teachings' rather than lessons, because as adults we grow through our own experiences, rather than being taught lessons by others).

I have tuned in to the energies of the stories, the land, nature spirits and spirit itself and have worked with them in a positive, life-enhancing way. These are my teachings which have been confirmed and strengthened by the shamanic work and by my experiences over the years. I have seen how others have grown through this work, taking on their stories, becoming inspired and enriched, connecting again with their ancestors and with the ancestral patterns and memories that lie there.

This is my life's work. These are my teachings. May they never be forgotten again.

Women's Ways – Ancient Roots

The women's way is to come together and share pain, grief, joy, laughter and fear.

In Ireland, our oral tradition has always fed us. It is part of the fabric of our land. Storytelling is what people do when they sit around in the evening. In country pubs, after a few drinks, people tell stories and sing songs. That is how we held our stories. History is written by the conquerors so it is his story. The oral tradition holds more of her story. These stories have been passed down through generations. They move us from longing into belonging and enable us to find self.

When I was young, I sat by the fire with Granny and her friends and they told stories. They usually waited until the men went out. Then, the whole dynamic changed. Chairs were pulled around the fire and the stories came. I was captivated by them and they were very sacred to me. The older women wanted to make sure I had the stories. Mrs Leary, especially, told her stories over and over. She always asked, "Do you have it now?"

In bed at night, I was still in the stories. I became the characters and could feel them alive around me. Now, I know that it was the memories in my blood being awakened. In Ireland, our stories hold parts of the memories of who we are and where we come from. If we open ourselves and allow the stories of our people to merge and flow through us, they can awaken ancient memories, knowledge and understandings within us and can inspire us on our life's path.

As women we have the capacity to hold each other in our stories and hold each other's stories. That is the most sacred of sacred.

When women share together and hold each other magic begins to happen. Things shift and change. What one woman goes through, we all feel. When we are open, we go through it with her. Rather than taking from her, that honours her experience. By holding her experience within ourselves, we can hold her. We can grieve or laugh with her. Our role is to be the sister who holds her, knowing that, another day, she will be the one who holds us.

It is a natural function for us, as women, to move into the sacred together, to support each other and to midwife through birth, death, pain and joy. When a woman gives birth, other women are usually with her. In the tradition of the bride and bridesmaid, the bridesmaid shares with her and holds her when she goes through that transition. When a woman faces the death of a lover or family member, other women gather and bring food to her door. They sit with her, hold her hand and listen to her stories. It brings them into the sacred.

Ritual grows from and through honouring those pivotal times in our lives that have moved or changed us. When we are able to express those experiences through ritual, we can find closure. A ritual allows us an outward expression of what we hold within ourselves.

The Yes Woman

By following the Way of the Seabhean (yes woman), we say yes to life and to what is thrown at us. Yes, let's go for it! Let us eat and drink of life rather than being observers. We do this in the way of the hundreds of thousands of women who have walked this path before us. The Way of the Seabhean is a path of power, passion and grace.

We are brought up to fear our power as women and to give it away to the priest, the doctor, the teacher, our father or our husband. On this path, we reclaim our power.

Passion is life force. It is our fire. Awakening to being passionate about anything – nature, dance, music, movements to bring about change – or passion for life itself activates that life force and lets us know that, indeed, we are alive! It is the presence of grace that enables us to hold our space.

Women have always sat in circles together. They often find their own personal power when they sit in circles with other women.

All over the world women are fighting to be heard and to be seen as equals in their work and in their lives. We carry within us the desire to stand in our power as women. To do this, we can draw on our own, inner seabhean. This is our opportunity to stand in our proper place in and upon this world. We have the word 'Sea! and we use it. We are saying Yes! By saying that, we build up positive energy. Yes, we will take back our power. Yes, we will live in our authenticity. Yes, we are women and we do not try to be other than what and who we are, in our sacredness and wildness.

When we say that 'Sea! we recognise our power, strength and

passion. We also recognise the grace that lies within us. We have been reclaiming all of that since the time of the suffragettes. Our power as women is becoming stronger as time goes by. We have had our setbacks but women are rising now, all across the world.

Women are rising again to reclaim what is theirs by natural right. When we speak our truth and claim our rights, we do that for all women. That affects all, because we are interconnected.

By following the Way of the Seabhean, we allow ourselves to step right into the centre of our own fire, our own passion. We awaken to that presence of fire within us and dance in that fire. We own and use it, rather than fearing it.

Reclaiming

On the path of the seabhean, part of our work is accessing ancient memories, the memories of our grandmothers, their grandmothers and their grandmothers before them. The mitochondrial DNA carries knowledge that comes through our foremothers, connecting us back through time and space. Such richness we carry in our DNA! We can reclaim direct memories through the woman's line. Standing on the shoulders of our foremothers, we can draw through them. They hold us, whisper to us and encourage us.

In the arcane teachings, as we reclaim our fire and awaken our passion, the fire shifts from the base chakra (kundalini) and moves up into the flame of the heart. That passion becomes compassion. We can dance in our fire, embrace our passion and also move into that place of compassion. As women, that is essential to us. Our natural tendency is to go into the place of sympathy and empathy where we can take on energies that do not belong to us. When we move into compassion we recognise the pain another is going through. We can stand with them, support them and be at their back, but we cannot take it from them and on to ourselves, either consciously or unconsciously. Some people want us to take that from them and, if we do, we disregard their soul's intention. Their soul needs them to grow through that to become self-empowered. The greatest gift we can give another is to allow them to go through that process without interference.

On the Way of the Seabhean, some might be seers or healers, some might hold sacred space or conduct rituals. Others might use the Way of the Seabhean to embrace all that they are and were meant to be.

The seabhean path is a way of reclaiming all that we are, bringing back the seabhean, the yes woman, and those memories that lie in our DNA. We are not staying silent any more. The Way of the Seabhean is not just a personal part of our lives, it also holds the balance of the weave. As we grow and open, we bring that into the weave of the earth.

THE WEAVE

Tbe world is a weave of energy
and every human being is a thread on that Great Weave. Each one of us is born with our own, unique canvas which, as yet, has no threads upon it. The pattern with which we are born is our soul's blueprint for what we need in this life and it will attract all the experiences, situations and relationships that we need to grow through. Every experience we have is a thread that brings colour and texture to our weave.

We can imagine our weave like a mediaeval tapestry. Women spent lifetimes embroidering those complex cloths which often told stories of great events. Our personal weave holds our stories and also colours the Great Weave of the earth.

Before we are born, our soul has agreements and contracts with other souls. It has chosen the family it needs to come through in order to grow. Some people find that difficult. They ask, "You mean I chose this (dysfunctional) family?" The soul has chosen that family because it knows what it needs and it creates scenarios to grow through. It may also have chosen a role to release ancestral patterns in that family.

The vibration of the soul creates an energy body to attract all that it needs when it comes into this life. Our weave attracts people, situations and experiences.

Our personal weave also colours the great fabric of energy that is part of the living breath of the earth and all upon the earth. Each one of us is a pivotal point on the Great Weave. As on a spider's web, each point is connected to others. A vibration in one part of the web causes a resonance throughout. Every experience we grow through, everything we open to and move through, affects the Great Weave of the earth. As we grow, awaken and evolve in life, we imprint that on the Great Weave, so that others, experiencing similar situations, can draw energetically from our imprint to assist them. We can also draw, energetically, from others' growth and understanding. Those connections and experiences bring life and colour to our personal weave too.

We affect the whole. What an amazing, mind-blowing realisation that is. Everything is electromagnetic – our actions, words, thoughts, daydreams, fantasies and emotions. We are part of this magnificent fabric of energy that holds us all and affects us all too.

Often in life, there are situations, people or memories that we hold, because we do not want to let go of them. Any experience to which we are still connected emotionally, psychologically, physically or mentally, is like a thread that is pulled taut between the tapestry and ourselves, like a pulled thread on a piece of material. Every person with whom we have not had closure, is a pull on that tapestry. As long as those threads are still attached, we are unable to move beyond that experience. Those pulled threads will attract that, or similar experiences, into our lives again and again.

By holding on to people and things that pull our weave, we can block the way for new experiences, new situations and new people. Our fear of losing them and our fear of having to change who we are to accommodate their loss, can sometimes hold us back from becoming all that we are meant to be. By keeping a thread constantly pulled taut in one place, we negatively affect the entire weave.

In order to grow through and beyond that experience we need to cut the threads that no longer serve us. That process is called cutting the ties. Having cut the ties, we also need to release that experience consciously, so we do not attract it back into our lives again. If we release the thread and keep our own weave in balance, we can help to balance the Great Weave.

Once we understand the weave, how it works and how we can participate in it, rather than resisting or being passive to it, that sets us on a path. We begin a path of consciousness.

Imagine each one of us consciously focusing on positive, creative, beautiful, loving, peace-filled thoughts and feelings and those billions of atoms of energy flowing forth from each one of us becoming the living impulse of our weave and of the Great Weave. By imagining and feeding into this, we can begin to make it happen.

The more conscious we become in making choices, the more we exercise free will and the more we follow our true path. If we listen to the call of our own soul nature that echoes through us, we will always be in the right place in our lives and moving ever forward. It is rare to have a straight path. We walk a spiral path so that we can gather all the experiences and understandings that we need.

When we have finished working on our weave and our tapestry is complete, we move on again from this life. Our souls go forth, home again, filled with those experiences and understandings. If anything has not been completed or understood, or anything has been denied, the thread will remain taut and that vibration will continue to attract those teachings/lessons in our other lives, or it may become an ancestral pattern in the lives of those who come after us.

Each one of us is responsible for keeping the earth, our Great Mother, in balance. In the work I do, with myself, individuals and groups, my main focus is to bring balance to my own weave and the weaves of others, as this will help keep the Great Weave in balance. Out of all the teachings and all the work, our role in balancing the Great Weave is the most important.

Balancing the Weave

The intention of shamanic work is to hold the weave together, to hold the balance of the weave, whether we see it as dragon lines, ley lines, or as a huge web. For me, it is a weave. It is energy. We change energy simply by being within it. Even if we stand in an empty room, we change the dynamics of that room by our energy.

If there are others in the room, they are affected by our energy, just as we are affected by theirs. To balance the weave, we need to be aware of sharing positive energy and of protecting ourselves, so we do not pick up negative energies that are not ours.

The more we connect and the more we become conscious of the

weave and our role within it, the more we can harmonise the whole. The essence of the teachings is to balance the weave. When the weave is in balance, life, the earth and the person is in balance.

The Roles of the Seabhean

As we progress on the Way of the Seabhean, some of us will choose a path of walking between the worlds, being able to move betwixt and between. Some will find their role holding space and creating ceremony. Others will express the way through dance and sounding. A few will include all of these in their path.

Traditionally, when a child was ill, the tribe had a person who journeyed into the child's weave to see what was not in balance, what was pulling or taking from their energy, or what was trying to intrude into their weave. Some of us might become seabhean practitioners or "healers" in this way.

As shamanic practitioners, it is not our intention to heal people. There is a big difference between the shamanic practitioner and a spiritual healer, reiki practitioner or any other type of healer.

The type of shamanic healing that we do is to help to bring balance to the weave. Each person is a weave within themselves. When we feel, sense, scan, drum or rattle on another, we sense their weave around them. We work to help them recognise what is out of balance and can work with them to rebalance that. Our work involves removing things that are taking energy from people, retrieving bits of them that they have lost or left along the way and weaving rips or holes in the fabric of their energetic bodies. It is not our role to cure them. What we can do is balance their weave so that it can support them in curing themselves or, occasionally, so that they can move on with ease from this life, if that is meant to be.

If someone comes to me and is dying of cancer, I might 'see' that they are already moving or disconnecting from their body. Then, it is not my role to cure them. Is it a cure to keep them alive in pain or on drugs? My role could be to help prepare them. I could talk to them, find out what regrets they have or what stories they want to share, what they want to be remembered by and whether there is anyone to whom they need to say something. If that person is no longer in their lives, I could ask them what they would say if the person were here. This is what the weave calls for: to release the bonds that are holding them. My role is to recognise the balance of their weave and to respond to that. All of that helps to balance their weave. When their weave is in balance it harmonises with the weave of our living, breathing earth.

Another part of the seabhean role can be to tune into the energy in the ground and feel when there is an imbalance there. We can then do energy work to help balance it. That could involve putting down crystals, blessing the waters, praying and chanting, or whatever needs to be done to bring it back into balance.

As more women are trained as shamanic practitioners in the Way of the Seabhean, we can also contribute to the greater picture. Through our consciousness, through our understanding of the weave, we can become like a standing wave. We can learn to channel energies through us so that, wherever we stand, we connect energies through us into the earth.

Dreamers, Weavers and Soulsingers

Near Rathmore in County Kerry, not far from where I live, lie The Paps of Anu. The Paps are naturally shaped like two, beautiful, big breasts and ancient people built cairns on the top of each, like nipples on the Great Mother's breasts. The Great Mother was known as Ana, the Tuath Dé called her Anu and, later, the Celts called her Danu.

Beside the Paps is an ancient enclosure called The City – *Cathair Crobh Dearg* (Red Claw's Enclosure). Archaeologists believe that the sacredness of this site (and the Paps, beside it) accounts for the absence of other monuments in the area around it. It is thought to be the oldest place of worship of the Great Mother in Europe.

At The City, in the inner sanctum, they found artefacts of ritual, which belonged only to women. In the second ring, there were artefacts of ritual that belonged to men and women. From the third ring out, they found artefacts that belonged to the community – fragments of cooking pots, flint and things of that nature. They surmised that it was a matrifocal rather than a matriarchal tradition. Matriarchal traditions worship the feminine, the goddess and/or the earth and only women can be intermediaries between the people and the goddess. In a matrifocal tradition, men and women worship the goddess, and men also hold positions (not necessarily the top positions). The City had a matrifocal tradition.

The Paps of Anu, County Kerry

I have taken many groups there over the years, retrieving information and stories. Part of the information that was gifted to me in that place was that, as priestesses, the women there had different roles. They were dreamers, weavers or soulsingers, so they could dream weave or sing/sound things into reality. Each woman had one of those roles that was stronger than the others.

Traditionally, most indigenous cultures had people who could dream for the clan or tribe. They could go into darkness, or quietness, to dream and then tell the tribe what was needed. If someone was sick, they could tell them what was wrong with them. When the tribe or the clan needed to move to better hunting grounds, they could dream where that was to be.

The dreamers are little recognised in today's world. At school, children are trained not to daydream. Schools are focused on developing the intellect to the point where children lose their natural ability to attune to other levels and realms.

Weavers are often solution-oriented people. Sometimes they use energies to bring harmony and continuity. They can weave the threads together when they have been loosened or released. In telling stories, they can weave their clan and their people together. We weave our lives around us to create a place of safety, a web to fall into which will hold us safe. People can also create webs that cause distrust and dependency.

Soulsingers use sound to sing into reality that which they wish to create. In the beginning was sound. People in India have worked with sound for over four thousand years. Everything has a frequency, a vibration. Our bodies have a sound and each organ in our bodies is a harmonic of that sound. Sound can clear energy. It can attract. Without even seeing a person, we can be attracted to their voice.

Each one of us is part dreamer, part weaver and part soulsinger. We carry all three and can use them to create what we need. Usually, one is stronger than the other two. It is good to note which one that is for us.

Whatever role we may find for ourselves on the Way of the Seabhean, it is an easy step to begin the journey. Once we begin to imagine it, we have embarked on the path.

My bones still remember the freedom of life's dance.

My blood still tastes the sweetness of my choices.

And, in the silence of my hidden screams, my foremothers whisper 'awaken, arise and reclaim all that you are meant to be.'

I am She

I am me

I am you.

Witch, wild and tender. Mother, strong and holding. Child, innocent and open. Cailleach, knowing and rebellious to the end.

WALKING
BETWEEN THE
WORLDS

Three Main Worlds

IN OUR TRADITION WE HAVE THREE MAIN WORLDS THAT are best explained by the image of a tree. Our Lower World is the place of our ancestors, our Middle World is our present reality, here and now, and our Upper World is the place of spirit. The Lower World can be likened to the roots of the tree, the Middle World to the trunk and the Upper World to the branches. The height and width of those branches is mirrored almost exactly by the depth and spread of the roots, most of which are underground.

As we do not see those roots, we often forget about them. People want to go up, to go out, to move towards the light. Unless we have those roots holding us down in the depths, strong, deep and solid, we will fall over because we are not grounded. A tree cannot grow if its roots are not strong.

Throughout my years, I have attuned and journeyed shamanically with trees, going down into their roots. In that way, the trees revealed themselves to me as the symbol for the Lower, Middle and Upper Worlds.

Tree of Life (The Three Realms)

Upper World
> Branches
> Place of Spirit

Middle World

> Trunk
> Place of Being
> This Reality

Lower World
> Roots
> Place of Power/Ancestors

Lower World, Place of Power and the Ancestors

The Lower World, our roots, is our place of power because it is the place of our ancestors and we carry our ancestors in us, in our bones and our blood. We carry their memories and stories. Knowing what we carry gives us power.

Our ancestors are the roots that ground us and hold us here on the earth. In my work, we always begin with the Lower World because we cannot do any more work if we are not grounded. What holds us here if we are not grounded? The first part of knowing who we are is knowing who our people were. That is a great Irish tradition. The old folk always wanted to know, "Who are your people?" They were asking who our ancestors were.

Traditionally, at Samhain (October 31st) in Ireland, people sat around the fire and told stories of their ancestors. They knew who they were and the roots from which they came. The sense of our ancestors is strong within us. We are here because our ancestors survived over seven hundred years of invasions. With their strength, tenacity, courage, beliefs and love, they survived famines, wars and loss.

People come home to Ireland in search of their roots. When people feel rootless, they have difficulty grounding themselves, being at ease or finding peace within themselves. Sometimes those roots can be miles, or continents, away from the people they grew up with. People often need to travel back to their ancestral roots and let go of something that they carry, before they are able to grow on.

Many people come to Ireland consciously, aware of coming to the land of their foremothers and forefathers who left because of famine, war or poverty, knowing that they would never return. We lost three-fifths of our population during and around the Great Famine of 1847. Of those who left, many went to North America and more died aboard the 'coffin' ships.

It is said that Irish emigrants put earth into their pockets. The ache of leaving their motherland, forever, was so harsh that they carried small pieces of home with them.

Generations later, people who carry that ache are now returning. When they come back consciously, walk upon the earth of their homeland and feel the pulse of her nature (which is so strong in Ireland), many cry. Many fall to the ground and hug the earth, not knowing why they do it.

Some years ago, in the Killarney National Park, I met a man from Chicago and he was crying. He was embarrassed and did not know why he was crying. I said to him, "You are crying because your people cried when they left and you are bringing them home. Your tears, your DNA is going back into the land, so you are bringing them home." He went to the National Park officials and asked if he could plant a tree in honour of his family and they said of course he could. After he did, he felt a space in his heart that he had never felt before. Something shifted, something left him.

Our ancestors, male and female, live within us. Their DNA is in our build or colouring, we also carry it deep within our memories, in our bones and our blood. We carry their memories and stories within us. It is just that we have forgotten them. Often, if we listen to the elders in our family telling the stories, we can feel them and, sometimes, begin to see them, because the stories remind us of what we already carry.

In our tradition children were given names of an ancestor, often one who had passed on. People carry names belonging to aunts, uncles, grandfathers and grandmothers. The name has power and energy: it holds memories of those people and invokes their energy.

In Inuit, Yupic and certain African tribes, they believe that, when they give a child the name of an ancestor, they invoke the memories of that ancestor. Some of those tribes treat the child as if it were the ancestor. People come and say, "Great to see you, I haven't seen you for forty years." Anthropologists have found that those children have started remembering: they have memories that are actually memories of the ancestors themselves. They can access those memories in their DNA.

Our roots hold us deep down into and through the earth. Like a tree, we grow from our roots, because those roots feed us. We also carry ancestral patterns embedded in our roots, patterns that can often go back through generations. Some of those are healthy, strong patterns that support, feed and strengthen us. Others can pull at us, draw from us, drain or weaken us. Patterns that draw from us can often wrap themselves around healthy roots that are trying to feed and sustain us. This weakens us in our everyday life (Middle World) and keeps us in survival mode.

In our tradition, as in many shamanic traditions, we believe that if an ancestor passes on without completing their cycle or clearing everything they carry, that pattern stays in the family. Situations that did not have closure in our ancestors' lives, become patterns that move through generations, until somebody in that family blood line chooses to work through those patterns and release them.

It is good to know what we carry from our ancestors. Much of what we carry is strong and good, it has got us to where we are. Each of us is a product of thousands. Every one of them was sufficiently strong and te-nacious to survive all the hardships, so that each generation got stronger.

There can also be negative patterns. Alcoholism is a huge one and when it is not dealt with, it can pass down through generations as dif-ferent forms of addiction, for example, drug-addiction, sugar cravings or victim roles. Control is a pattern, especially in women who had to be subservient outside the house, so they took control within it. That was a very Irish pattern. It is important to recognise those patterns, work with them, process them and release or transform them.

Some women deal with their fears by nurturing others. That can be an ancestral pattern. Another common one is melancholy. In Ireland, this was often hidden. There is collusion in families. Many things are hidden and that, too, goes down through the generations.

Grief can be ancestral. I worked with a woman who suffered deep grief and could not understand why. She felt shame and was self-con-scious about it, although she never let people know. We did some work together and I journeyed with her. Her grandmother's mother had a child out of wedlock and the family was ashamed. She had to go and live with a maiden aunt. The baby died. She came back to the village and it was never mentioned again, as if the child had never existed. That grief went down into her womb, into the next child she carried, and into the next generation.

The woman researched and found that her great-grandmother had, indeed, left the village at the age of seventeen and had come back at nineteen, although nobody knew where she had gone or what had happened. This corroborated what we had found on the journey. I suggested that we do a ritual and she planted a flowering shrub in honour of that child. She felt much better afterwards. It was as if something in her had lifted. She had needed to go back to find what was holding her.

We have all caught ourselves saying or doing things like our mothers did. When I am tired, I tend to clean the kitchen instead of going to bed. My mother always did that. She could not go to bed until the kitchen was clean and the floor was washed or brushed. We carry patterns from our mothers.

Over the years, I have worked with about half a dozen people who were adopted. Because of the work we were doing, most of them went back and found the families into which they were born. They found that the patterns they carried were tied up with the birth families and were amazed at how similar these family patterns were. It is there in the DNA!

Some patterns are easy to recognise. Others can be difficult to see. Because we cannot see them, it does not mean that we do not have them – they can be hidden or covered.

Many ancestral patterns are instinctive and we fall back into them when we are tired, stressed, tense, or not breathing properly. We do not think about them, we just re-act instinctively. A reaction is an action replay that happens again and again. It could be with a different person, or different situation, but the playing out is the same. That pattern often goes back through generations. Instinctive patterns are sometimes the hardest ones to get hold of.

Sometimes a person, often a woman, is quiet about things and her mother and grandmother were like that too. Our shamanic work involves going back and finding out what closed down the voices in that matrilineal line, so we can see how to heal that. How can we open that now, so that the voices can be heard and that woman can be heard, seen and recognised? Often, if people do not give voice, they feel that they are not seen either. When they give voice, they begin to hold their power and stand in the middle of their world and their weave. Once they do that, they are seen and heard. They balance their weave.

Some years ago, a woman from Dublin came to me. She was born when her mother was forty. In her thirties, she could not get pregnant and adopted a child. At forty, she had a child of her own. When I met her, her birth daughter, who was then forty, rang to tell her that she was pregnant. It was such an obvious pattern over three generations! Some are not so easily recognised.

People often do not want to look at what they hold in honour of their ancestors. Unless we recognise them, those patterns will affect everything we do in life, because they are part of our roots. No matter how difficult they are, we have taken on those programmes or patterns in honour of our ancestors. Working in the Lower World allows us to see what we are carrying. We do not always need to know the story of where the pattern started. Sometimes, all that is needed is a ceremony or ritual to honour that pattern, as a way of releasing it.

Once we know what we carry in honour of our ancestors, even if we have not cleared it, it gives us power. Then, we can be true to who we are and what we carry. Nothing is negative. It is the way we allow that to move through us, or do not deal with it, that makes it negative.

As souls, we choose the family into which we are born. It is no mistake. Before we come into this world, we choose our family and the ancestral patterns through which we need to evolve, so that we can grow in this life. We knew, as souls, that we could change some of those ancestral patterns and release their imprint within the DNA of that bloodline for generations to come.

Once a person works through a pattern and releases it, everything shifts. The change in that family can either be dramatic or unobtrusive. That pattern is then released for all of their blood line: uncles, aunts, cousins, nephews, nieces, grand-nephews, grand-nieces, children, grandchildren, brothers, sisters and those yet to be born. The rest of the family can shift accordingly. After it is cleared, it is no longer instinctive. It becomes a choice rather than a pattern. They now have the opportunity to make that step, if they have not been able to do it before. Some family members might still choose to hold on to the pattern, depending on how that pattern 'feeds' them.

In my personal shamanic journeying with trees, they showed me how to journey down to my ancestors in the Lower World. The trees showed me that my ancestors still walk with me and are part of the living breath around me. They showed me that the bones of the ancestors become part of the living earth from which everything grows. The roots of the trees, the flowers, the vegetables and the grass that feeds the animals, all draw from the bones of our people. Our ancestors are in everything that is alive. I have since learned that this is part of our ancient teachings in Ireland. Before the coming of the Celts, the gods and goddesses of our land, the Tuath Dé, believed that, when our souls went forth to Tír na nÓg, our spirits became part of the living fabric of the land around us and that our physical bodies went into the earth to feed all, as we had been fed.

When our tree brethren send out the oxygen that we need to breathe and stay alive, we also breathe in our ancestors. To connect and commune with my ancestors, the trees showed me that I must journey down through their roots.

Journeying, as I was shown, allows us a rich opportunity to draw upon what lies deep within us. Coupled with our innate understandings, journeying awakens memories that we carry from our ancient Irish and Celtic ancestors. We are re-membering from and through them, within our own DNA.

Many of our stories have been lost or forgotten and part of the role of our elders was always to remind us of who we were and what we carried. What stories and gifts of knowledge they can share with us still, if we open to listen! Journeying to the Lower World gifts us that opportunity to listen, to ask questions, to know who we are and where we came from.

We journey to the Lower World to recognise our patterns and where they come from and to release patterns that restrict or no longer serve us. At times, we may journey to the Lower World when certain experiences keep repeating in our lives and we cannot fathom why. Why do I always attract that type of person into my life? No matter how hard I work, why do I never have money? We can journey to the Lower World, find our ancestral teacher and ask, what is in the family that is causing this to happen?

On a Lower World journey we encounter our ancestral totem and ancestral teacher. Our Lower World totem, our animal helper, is the totem of our clan or tribe. We all come from tribal people and every tribe had its own totem, whether it was a fox, an eagle, a hawk, a salmon, or any other animal. It was one of the most important things that the early Celts took into battle. Somebody carried a banner with that totem and led them into the battlefield. If that person fell, somebody else had to pick up that banner.

The totem that we have in our Lower World always appears on one of our ancestral families' shields. It can be on our mother's or father's family shield or our parents' or grandparents' shields, or further back, but it will definitely be there. For example, I am a Leinster Murphy – my father was from Wexford. The totem on the Leinster Murphy's shield is a lion and the words are 'brave and hospitable'. For much of my life, I had little to do with the lion but, at a point when somebody was directing extreme, negative energy at me, the lion came immediately to protect me. Since then, my lion is often beside me and I know that I can call upon him whenever I am in need. He is always just a breath away. Many people meet their ancestral totem first through journeying and later find it on their family shield.

Our ancestral teacher is one of our ancestors who has passed over, part of our bloodline, blood of our blood. For an Irish person, this ancestor will be Irish, unless we have ancestry from other countries. We cannot pick and choose our ancestral teachers. We go to the ancestor that we need to connect with for what we need to work through. It is not necessarily a grandparent or a great-grandparent. Sometimes the imprint of our DNA is in alignment with somebody who could be five, or seven, generations back. It could be somebody we never knew, but we might have a strong connection with them because of energies or similarities that we carry.

Journeying to the Lower World

We all know the story of *Alice in Wonderland* by Lewis Carroll. It is archetypical of the myth of going into the unconscious. We journey into our own DNA through the symbolism of our roots. This is our Lower World.

When you embark on a Lower World journey, the question that you carry is your quest. What question do you want to carry into the Lower World, to ask of your ancestors? If you have not journeyed before, I recommend asking, "What patterns do I carry through or from you, which need to be released? And how may I release them?" Before you look for anything for yourself, it is important to recognise what you carry. Owning what lies within you brings truth and clarity into your life.

The question I recommended is for people who have never journeyed before, but there might be another question, to do with your ancestors, which is aching for you to resolve. You may want to understand where a pattern is coming from and how to release it. Where it comes from can be secondary to how you release it, although sometimes you cannot release it unless you know. The answer will depend on your ancestral teacher. You need not worry if they focus on one side rather than the other.

You write down your question clearly and simply. The clearer the question, the clearer the answer, always. If it is convoluted with part one, two and three, the response may not be obvious.

To journey, you need to make time and quiet space for approximately thirty minutes. Lying down is best, unless you are drumming or likely to fall asleep. You need a blanket or cover for your body. Traditionally in Ireland, people wove feathers, especially heron feathers, into a shawl to wear for journeying. You need a scarf or bandana to cover your eyes. The scarf assists in closing off this reality.

For a Lower World journey, you usually use a drum. This drumming prevents your mind from getting in the way of the journey. The speed of the drum affects the brain and stops you from thinking and creating your own reality. The drum lets you know when the journey has ended and it is time to come home. You can do your own drumming, pre-record it, or choose one of the many recordings available online, to follow as you journey. It is important to have a book and pen to record your journey as soon as you can, after you return. As you become more proficient in journeying, you can look back at your notes and see how far you have come with the process.

When the drumming begins, you relax your body and make sure that you feel comfortable, safe and warm. Then, in your mind's eye, you take yourself to a 'place of safety', a physical place that you know, somewhere in nature that moves you and where you are at peace within yourself. It could be beside a waterfall, lake or stream. In that place you can see, feel and hear the sounds of nature around you: birds singing, wind blowing through the trees, the sound of crickets, or silence. You might feel the sunshine on you, or a warm breeze touching you gently as you sit and lean against something, a stone or a tree. Sitting in the shade or in the sun, you feel the solidity of that stone or tree at your back. This is 'your' place and, through constant journeying, it becomes sacrosanct to you. I usually recommend to people not to choose a place by the sea because the sea has a very strong magnetic quality that can make it difficult to journey to the Lower World.

From your sacred space, you journey downwards into the Lower World. If you are sitting beside a tree, you could find yourself going down through the roots. Leaning by a stone, you might find that the ground opens up, or you could go down through a cave.

Going down into the Lower World can often feel like a corkscrew, going round and round, down and down. Sometimes you just feel yourself dropping down. For one man, it was an escalator. It is important to go with whatever works for you, as you go down into this Lower World, on your quest, carrying your question with you.

I suggest that you use a door to enter the Lower World, until you are comfortable and used to journeying there. (You will later close this door when you leave.) In my workshops (and on the recorded journey available on my website), I talk you down into the Lower World and you journey alone from there, accompanied only by the drumbeats. That is the big difference between a guided meditation and a shamanic journey.

The Lower World is what many call the misty world, the land of shadow where the ancestors dwell. It is not vibrant like the world of colour that we have here: the colours are toned down and dull.

First, you call your ancestral totem to you and an animal should come to you, whether it is four-legged, eight-legged, many-legged, has wings or fins, or whether it slithers along the ground. Whatever it is, an animal helper will come when you call them. You ask them, "Are you my ancestral totem?"

If they say, "No, but I have come to help," you say, "I really thank you for that and I need to call my ancestral totem".

You need to be quite clear that that is your ancestral totem. While you are very grateful to any other ally that comes to help and support you, you are looking for your ancestral totem. That clarity is important.

Sometimes the totem comes in before you know it. People say, "Oh I saw a spider, but I was thinking I have to find my ancestral totem." Actually, the spider might have been their totem. You need to be aware of what is there and what comes to you before you even think of calling out. Sometimes the totems are just waiting to pop in and share with you. What that totem means to you is quite specific. A spider might mean something for one person and something different for another. You need to be open to the totem that is there and not reject it.

Afterwards, you can think and feel into what that totem means to you personally. What do you think about that animal, insect or bird? What gift do you feel it brings to you? For example, the spider brings deep gifts: it builds a web, traps flies and also sheds its skin. A spider's web holds things together. The spider shows you how to balance things.

The gift of the mouse is to move quickly. It has to see what is around it, so the mouse is telling you to look at what surrounds you, to be awake and aware. Then the eagle, flying high, has to see for a great distance. So there is a huge difference between the mouse and the eagle.

It is interesting to recognise the gifts that each totem brings to you.

There are books that explain what these animals mean, yet it is important to find what it means to you personally, rather than somebody else's interpretation. This totem has come to you and its specific meaning is for you to understand.

When you meet your ancestral totem, you ask them to take you to your ancestral teacher and, when you feel, see, or sense someone with you, or when your totem takes you to meet them, you ask, "Are you my ancestral teacher?"

You have to have that clarity because, sometimes, other ancestors, Uncle Mick or Great-Aunt Kathleen, may pop in. If they say, "No, but I want to have a chat," you can reply, "Thank you, but I am looking for my ancestral teacher; you are welcome to come along."

Then, you call out again for your ancestral teacher to join you. When you confirm that this is your ancestral teacher, you ask them their name, because the name invokes power and energy. Knowing their name strengthens your connection to them.

I remember one person saying, "I got this teacher but I could not believe she was my teacher because she was old and moany, and I thought, I don't like her, I'll look around for someone else." It is important not to reject the teacher that comes to you.

Sometimes, people feel the ancestral teacher there but cannot see them as clearly as they would like. They just get a glimpse. One person kept seeing the teacher's back and followed them but could never catch up. She got irritated, threw out a question and got the answer, "Haven't you been looking at the path?" When she looked down, the answer was on the path and she had been walking on it. It took quite a few journeys for her to see the face. People might see the face or the body. It comes in different ways.

What if you do not have a guide and nobody comes? Everybody has an ancestral guide. You have ancestors: two parents, four grandparents, sixteen great-grandparents, thirty-two great-great-grandparents and further back. Trust me, there is at least one.

Sometimes, you can have difficulty in perceiving your ancestral teacher because you have a block. Everyone carries baggage and, if you do not know what luggage you have, your journey can reflect that and may be impeded. You need to know what you carry into the journey. Often, people who are brought up in a specific belief structure are blocked because they feel that they should not go into the Lower World. On some level, they feel that this is wrong or evil. Even though they do not believe it anymore, that might have become a subconscious pattern. It has become so ingrained that they are not even aware of it. You need to acknowledge that this place, to which you are going, is safe and good and that the energy, that you ask to join you, is benign and there to assist you. Your teachers are always there to aid you. In the forty years I have been working, I have never encountered evil on a Lower World journey and I give thanks for that.

The question carries you, so it has to be clear and concise. On your first journey into the Lower World the quest has to do with what ancestral programmes you are carrying and how you may release them.

You ask the question of your ancestral teacher and see, feel, sense or hear the answer. It could be all or just one of the above, depending on which senses work best for you. The Irish are generally visual people, so we tend to see it. That is not the case for everyone. For example, when my artist friend Helen journeys, she does not see the journey, she senses it. When she paints, she asks the Goddess to come to her and starts working when she feels the energy with her. She does not know what her hands will do, it just comes through her. You need to be aware that it will come in whatever way is most natural for you. When the ancestor shares with you and tells you what patterns you carry, then you ask, "What is the best way to release this?" It is important not to be vague.

The drumming changes when it is time to come back. When I drum in my workshops, I speed up, slow down and stop, or simply stop. Occasionally, I stop, then wait a couple of minutes, drum a little again and then stop. The change in drumming lets you know that it is time to prepare to return. That does not mean that you have to leave immediately.

It is important to thank your ancestral teacher for the gifts they have shared with you and ask that they might journey with you again and help you. You might give them a gift of something you have in your hand, or that you take from inside your body. They might give you a gift.

Then you do the same with your totem. You thank them for journeying with you and ask them to stay close to you in your life, so that you can get to know them. Again, they might give you a gift: a word, symbol, flower or crystal. It could be anything.

Gradually, you come back into your place of safety again, remembering to close the door behind you. You relax there for a few minutes, breathing in the beauty of that place, allowing yourself to be in that space, calm and at ease.

From your place of safety, you come gently back into this space of here and now. You rest for a few minutes. I strongly suggest that you do not jump up, but allow yourself to rest and feel that you are really back here. Become aware of your back, neck, feet and toes as you relax into your body again. Then, when you feel ready, you can sit up. It is important to make those transitions when returning, otherwise your energy is not fully in your body and you can feel a bit spacy afterwards.

I have recorded a Lower World journey which you may use for journeying. Visit: www.celticsouljourneys.com/seabhean-journeys/#lower

Benefits of Lower World Journeying

Once we have journeyed, have received answers and know what we carry, that gives us inner power and reserves to fall back on. We become more grounded, rooted and stable.

Our animal nature carries the programmes with which we were born. This is our instinct – how we react to things. When we begin journeying into the Lower World and connecting with our ancestors, we start to understand our instincts. We hear the message our instinct gives us, recognise and honour that message, but those instincts no longer control us.

Sometimes people leave countries and continents to get away from their ancestors or family, yet they carry those patterns with them in their weave. That will only change when they have dealt with those patterns that they carry in honour of their ancestors.

Our soul has chosen these roots for us. By journeying, we let go of some patterns that no longer serve us. As we continue this process, there will be others for us to deal with, until our roots are strong and healthy. We cannot judge ourselves for our unhealthy patterns because these are what our soul has chosen for us to work through.

Working with our patterns in the Lower World gives us healthy roots and stability, so we can journey on to the Middle and Upper Worlds. We are held in our roots and this brings us, time and again, home to self.

THE MIDDLE
WORLD

The Middle World is the trunk of the tree. It is the reality we live in now, our present time and place. We call it our place of being.

For each of us, our Middle World is our personal story. Our bodies reflect the experiences we grow through in life, just as trees, as they age, develop scars, growths and wrinkles on their trunks. As well as carrying our stories, we are our stories. Every line and fold in our body is part of our soul's journey.

What is most important in the Middle World is how we participate in life. Do we participate or do we cut off from life because we cannot deal with certain things, people, issues, the country's affairs, or the world's affairs? Many people do not participate in life. They flow with whatever happens, or do what they are told. Others are frightened to participate. That fear holds them back, so they do not live or operate in this place of being.

How do we live in this reality? Do we actually live, or do we just survive? Some people are not alive but asleep, dreaming their lives away. To participate in this world, we need to be fully present, here in this place and time. We need to be conscious: real, alive, awake and aware. There are times when we can dream or journey. That is all natural. But we need to stay here and be in this reality, where we are meant to be, for this time. We are here for a reason.

The Middle World is also our relationship with the earth. How connected and interwoven are we with the earth, the seasons and the movement of the ancient calendar, the Wheel of the Year? Do we recognise that the earth is our mother and has fed, watered us and cared for us? How do we do that for her now? Our stewardship of the earth is most important.

How do we create in this place of being? Do we actually create our reality or do we allow ourselves to be influenced by the creativity of others? If we do not create our own reality we will be part of someone else's. How do we want the world to be? We are here to create that. It was our choice to come into this world, in this place, in this country, at this time. We have been preparing for this for lifetimes, because we are needed here right now. We have tools within us and available to us in the Middle World to assist our Mother Earth. We are here to participate and to be creators and creatrixes.

The Middle World is our place of consciousness and the intellect. We have seen that the Lower World is the subconscious, the instinctive, and all to do with reaction – instant replay – that is generations old in some cases. Here in the Middle World, in the place of consciousness, we should be thinking, not reacting. When we work shamanically, we always start in the Lower World by looking at what is inside, what is deep within us that needs to be worked through. We recognise that. Then, we bring that up into the Middle World, where we bring our intellect into it and choose to change the pattern.

The intellect connects to the way we relate to the world and other people and the way we balance our animal nature. How do we embrace our animal nature? Do we give in to it, or do we accept that it is ours?

Are we conscious or cognisant and aware of living in this reality? Do we make choices consciously? How do we unfold? Are we able to attract what we need?

This reality is connected to the elements: fire, earth, air and water and the elementals, by which I mean fairies, nature spirits and all those that live betwixt and between, seen and unseen. It is connected to our belief structures, to the gods and goddesses that we attune to and that feed us. There are different deities that preside in the Middle World, depending on which soul group we feel part of. Many people pray to deities such as Jesus, Buddha, or Muhammed. My personal deity is the Goddess in her phase as the Great Mother and I am moving towards the Cailleach as I grow in age.

In this world, we carry programmes that are given to us verbally and non-verbally by society, school, parents, religion and economics. We have a belief structure around our right to create. What we believe about our creativity can restrict us from fully creating our environment.

There is an Irish Middle World journey called the immram (from the Irish *iomramh*), which is part of the oral tradition. It is a quest. We have several well-known stories about immrama to the Otherworld (Tír na nÓg – the land of the forever young).

When you embark on an immram, you never come back as you were. Oisín went to Tír na nÓg with Niamh of the golden hair. He wanted to return to Ireland, and she warned him not to dismount from his horse. When his feet touched the ground of Ireland, he became an old, old man.

Our personal journey through this reality is like an immram. As soon as we wake up and become conscious, we can never go back to sleep, even though we might want to. We can only go forward. As souls, we are capable of staying awake and making choices. It is important for all of us to have choices.

People are waking up at this time. All across the world, they are beginning to make choices. They are beginning to participate and want more power in making choices about their own lives, communities and countries. That is healthy.

There is a lot going on in this space of the Middle World. It contains myths, stories, storytelling and the bardic tradition. The stories of our tribe are embedded in us and hold us in this reality. The Way of the Seabhean, women's mysteries, rituals and rites of passage belong here. The middle realm is also connected to the trees and stones.

Following the shamanic path, we have many Middle World tools available, for example crystals for healing and tools for divination: tarots, runes, astrology and numerology. Shamanic work like cutting the ties, soul retrieval, house-clearing and land clearing is done from this reality.

We have totems in the Middle World as well. These helpers may be from the animal kingdom, known to us in the real world, or they may be elementals: fairies, leprechauns, dragons or mer-people. Sometimes our Middle World totems can be deities. They come to assist, protect or teach us and to awaken us to the other realms with which we share this living space. Many of our totems are just a breath away from us on a daily basis although we may not be aware of them. They often assist us by reflecting back aspects of ourselves. Usually, we are born with one that is specific to us and is with us throughout life. It could be a deer, horse, sparrow, mouse, mackerel, or even a dragon. Some children are born with fairies as their totems. They see fairies everywhere. Sometimes you see babies laughing when there is nothing there. Then the cat reacts because the cat sees it too.

Whereas our Lower World totems (with the exception of the griffin) are always from the animal kingdom and appear on our family crest, a Middle World totem can be any creature, real or imaginal, with which we have a connection. Maybe cats always came to us when we were young. The Middle World totems are not usually connected to our family of birth and blood. Instead, they are connected to what we need to understand of ourselves and our relationship to the Middle World. At a transitional time in our lives, another totem may step in and can stay with us. Up to three totems can walk with us and we can journey with them.

We also have allies in the Middle World. These are not just from the animal realm; they can also be from the elemental realm and from the plant kingdom, for example flowers or trees. An ally might be with us for a moment of time, to help us to understand something about ourselves or another. It could also be with us for five minutes, five days, or five years.

In our tradition, the Middle World also includes the Wheel of the Sun, which shares some similarities with the Native American medicine wheel. The Wheel is the greatest tool in this reality. It is there for us energetically, along with the goddesses and archetypes who are associated with it. The Wheel is what holds the Middle World together. It reflects our life's journey. We are always somewhere on the Wheel in our lives, work and relationships. The next section of the book will explore the Wheel in detail, from the perspective of the Irish tradition and specifically the Way of the Seabhean.

THE WHEEL
OF THE YEAR

In the story of Ireland, the Wheel of the year, traditionally called the "Wheel of the Sun", goes back throughout time. The symbol of the wheel is at Newgrange, Knowth, Loughcrew, Fourknocks and other sacred sites. It is an eight-spoked wheel and the four main points are: Samhain (October 31st), Imbolc (February 1st), Bealtaine (May 1st) and Lughnasa (August 1st).

Originally, according to our stories, these festivals were celebrated on the full moons nearest to those dates. After the Irish calendar changed to the Roman calendar, they moved to the dates which we now celebrate. Our Wheel celebrations always start in the evening and continue into the day. It was known that the seed grows from darkness into light and darkness is a time of power – being near to those who have passed before and connected to the places betwixt and between. They are celebrated over three days.

Our four lesser, static points are the equinoxes and solstices: spring equinox 21st March; summer solstice 21st June; autumn equinox 21st September and winter solstice 21st December (approximately).

The Wheel is a circle and the four main points are like an 'X' that is slightly larger than that circle. The other four points are like a '+' contained within it. Our four main ('X') points go outside the circle and move the Wheel while the other four points, the solstices and equinoxes, are static.

Each of our four main festivals: Samhain, Imbolc, Bealtaine and Lughnasa is a hinge, a movement from one season, place or space to another. Traditionally, the hinge was important in Irish culture. Turf (ancient peat from bogs, used as fuel for Irish hearthfires) was cut on three sides and turned over. The fourth side was the hinge. When we go through a door, the door has a hinge that moves us from one space to another. These points move the Wheel of the Year, to turn and turn again.

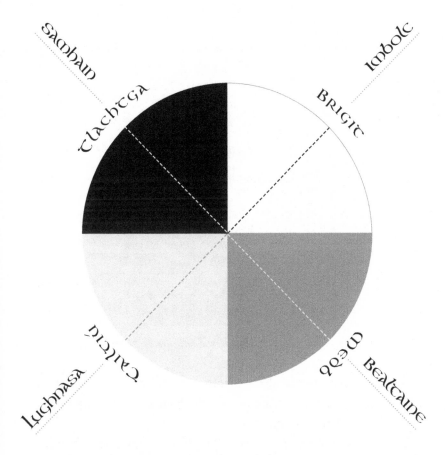

All four main points on the Wheel are fire ceremonies. In my Irish tradition, fire is the element of the Lower World. At each of these festivals, great fires were held in central locations and also in each province. Where I live, the Bealtaine fire is held beneath the Paps, in what is known as "The City". Lughnasa fires were held on a little island just off Cahersiveen and also in Cullen, County Cork. Locally, Lughnasa is celebrated by Puck Fair in Killorglin, whose dates are now set as the 10th, 11th and 12th of August. A wild puck goat is caught and crowned 'King of Ireland' for three days. They choose a young girl to be his 'consort' and she is crowned and carried around the town. The event is famous for its horse fair, music and celebration. The origins of Puck Fair go back through time as a harvest festival of Lughnasa.

King Puck in Killorglin, County Kerry. Sculpture by Alan Ryan Hall.

The four lesser points, the solstices and equinoxes, are the fixed points of east, south, west and north, which are the four main points on the Native American medicine wheel.

On the Irish traditional Wheel, fire is always in the South, because of the midsummer sun. Earth is always in the North. The elements of air and water can interchange depending on whether we live closer to the sea in the East or the West. If we live closest to the Atlantic, water is the element of the West on the Wheel. Closer to the Irish Sea, water is the element of the East.

The Archetypes

The Wheel is more than a calendar of our ancient festivals. There are archetypal deities associated with each of the eight points on the Wheel. Samhain is held by Tlachtga, Imbolc by Brigit, Bealtaine by Medb and Lughnasa by Tailtiú. The four lesser points are also held by deities/archetypes. Boann holds the spring equinox, Áine the summer solstice, Macha the autumn equinox and the Cailleach holds the winter solstice.

Some, like Brigit, Medb and the Cailleach are well known from traditional stories. Others, like Tlachtga and Tailtiú, less so. Each one of these deities took her own journey with me as I travelled the Wheel. Sometimes they stay with me for a few months, or, like Tlachtga, for a few years. With all the stories, I see them as if I am watching something on television. Sometimes I am observing and other times I am in the story. It can be both at the same time.

Whilst the better-known deities have historical counterparts that follow on from thousands of years of stories and practices, the lesser known deities have been almost completely lost. My work with the Wheel and the Way of the Seabhean has been in reclaiming them. I met Tlachtga and Tailtiú in journeys and saw where they came from before I had heard their names or visited their locations. In this chapter I will share with you both the practices and stories traditionally associated with these archetypes and festivals, alongside my own personal life journey, as an example to you of the Way of the Seabhean.

These deities go back thousands of years. And each of them holds an aspect of ourselves. We can walk the Wheel to see where we are in our lives and to understand and grow through our difficulties.

They are a reflection of us, as well as a presence unto themselves. The energy of Medb exists whether I believe in her, know about her, or not. She is there, an entity unto herself. Homage had been paid to the Goddess Medb long before the advent of Christianity. So the essence, the presence of Medb, lies deep within our psyche, within our blood and within the land. Once I begin to recognise her presence, I can begin to claim the part of me that is Medb.

If young girls were taught about the deities and played them out, they would play out all those different parts of themselves and begin to integrate them into their lives. Most of us were brought up to be only part of what we are. In today's world, especially in Christian and Muslim countries, women are taught to be submissive or passive and to personify the gentle energy that we associate with Tailtiú. If they could also embrace passionate Medb, go into the darkness of Macha to find themselves, open to the Cailleach's wisdom, find their place of beginning with Brigit, express their creativity through Boann and were allowed to let go of their burdens with Tlachtga, they would bring balance to their nature. It would bring a sense of being as one and allow them to draw on all, rather than part, of what they are.

SAMHAIN

Tlachtga

The two most powerful points on the Wheel are Samhain and Bealtaine. The year begins at Samhain, the gentle threshold between the light and the dark. It is the time when the veil is thinnest between us and the ancestors, which is why the Christian Church used it as the day of the dead, All Souls' Day.

The deity who presides over Samhain is the Goddess Tlachtga, a Munster goddess and daughter of Mog Ruith (Mog of the Wheel), the greatest magician this land has ever known. Stories of Mog Ruith go back way before the Celtic magician, Amergin. It is said that people were afraid to say his name aloud for fear of invoking him.

They lived on Valentia Island, in County Kerry, which had been gifted to Mog Ruith by the King of Munster as a reward for his assistance in defeating the King of Connacht. Both Mog Ruith and Tlachtga lived for a span of three to four hundred years.

Long before the coming of the Celts, they built a magical wheel called the "Wheel of the Sun" and on this wheel they journeyed into many worlds and many realities. It is said that Mog Ruith could shapeshift into a salmon, wolf, boar or hawk and that Tlachtga could shapeshift into a deer, raven, spider or wolf. They journeyed to different places on the earth and it is said that they were present in Rome for the death of Simon Magus, the magician whose clash with St Peter is recorded in the Bible (Acts of the Apostles 8:9-14).

Tlachtga had a great following of priestesses. One of her main schools was in County Meath on the Hill of Ward. She was also buried there. They now hold Samhain celebrations on the Hill of Ward.

Tlachtga holds the presence of Samhain and is the keeper of the gate between the worlds. She holds the hinge betwixt and between. Tlacht-ga teaches us the importance of releasing, of embracing death, before we can move on. Death does not often mean physical death, it means releasing. Only in releasing can we move forward. When we release something, we feel a lot lighter, energetically, within our bodies. If we are carrying something, we can feel heavy and dark within ourselves.

Tlachtga is the goddess who assists us when we work on soul mid-wifery (work on issues around physical death and how to prepare for it). When people are dying, or have passed over, we can bring that soul to Tlachtga, but we cannot go through the gate ourselves.

It can feel like we are going through darkness to reach Tlachtga. Often, we fear darkness, but the further we go, the more we realise that there is a small, steady light, way off in the distance. We just need to find that light and begin to follow it.

From our first breath we all move towards Tlachtga. It is to Tlacht-ga we all go eventually, when it is our time to pass through the gate. She whispers to us as we grow on in life and we can celebrate moving towards her, as death is not something to be feared: it is part of life. Fear of death makes us fear life and restricts our ability to truly live. We need to eat and drink of life. No matter where we go or what we do, she will be there to receive us at the end of our time on this earth. There is great power in knowing that.

By facing our mortality, we live from a place of peace and vitality. Being with death gives us life, recognising its beauty and value. The presence of Tlachtga is important for us to befriend in our lives.

Samhain Traditions

Traditionally, the year ended on 30th October and the new year be-gan on the 1st November. The day between, the 31st October, was a day of no year. It belonged to the ancestors. On Samhain (Hal-lowe'en) people took out items (pieces of cloth, clay pipes, combs or jewellery) that had belonged to their ancestors. These mementoes helped them to connect and commune with them.

People battened down doors and windows, getting ready for winter. They brought the cattle indoors, to survive the winter and to keep the people warm in the *bothán* (cottage). Farm work slowed down, so they had time to visit each other and share stories of those who had passed on.

Samhain carried people into the winter months when days were short and nights were long. It was a time of integrating all that had gone on in the working months, for contemplation and for finding inner balance.

At Samhain, they called on their ancestors for help. In sharing the stories of the year – who had died, married or been born – and the stories of their people, they allowed themselves to release what they were holding.

Colcannon was the food of Samhain – potato, cabbage and onion mashed together with cream and butter. Barm-brack is a traditional fruit cake containing raisins, soaked overnight in tea. The tradition was to add a farthing coin, a piece of cloth and a ring into the cake. Children waited anxiously to see if they would receive the farthing which meant they would be rich when they grew up, the piece of cloth which meant that they would be poor, or the ring which meant that they would marry. They often ate the cloth rather than admit that they had got it!

Turf (peat) is a symbol of Samhain and is part of our ancestry. According to our stories, Ireland was once a land of black oaks and apple trees. For thousands and thousands of years, the trees lived here in quiet relationship with the land and with the Stone People until the two-leggeds came. So the trees too, are our ancestors. Nearly a third of the land of Ireland is turf which holds the roots of the great, black oaks that have been sucked down into the earth. In recent centuries, turf has been used as fuel to keep us warm. It is rich in minerals. The turf kept the fire going all through the year, to smoke fish and meat for the winter, to cook food and to keep people warm. Turf is also a symbol of darkness and the colour of Samhain is black.

Samhain, the time of our ancestors, was the most important time of the year in Ireland, because the people believed, and still believe, that our ancestors walk with us and that we walk on their bones. Many of our ancestors died in the Great Famine and were never buried, so when we walk on the earth, we walk on the bones of our ancestors.

In the old tradition, when a person dies, a bee often comes and carries their soul to Tír na nÓg, the land of the forever young. Their spirit becomes part of the energy of the earth herself. So the air that we breathe, the colour of the flowers and the songs of the birds, all carry the energy of our ancestors. They are around us all the time.

A Personal Journey with Tlachtga

Tlachtga came to me before I returned to Ireland permanently. I was visiting Kerry and I went to a sacred well in Ballyheighue. It was a lovely day and I was sitting on Ballyheighue beach, eating an ice cream, when a raven came walking towards me, staring at me. I was unnerved, because the raven is associated with death. So, I broke off a piece of wafer and threw it as far as I could. The raven caught and ate it and walked back towards me. I kept doing this and I was getting more and more nervous. Eventually, the raven came right up to me, staring continually at me. It bothered me, so I left and drove home. That night, a poem came to me:

Returning to Source

She calls to me

And I answer.

She sings to me

And I dance.

She whispers to me

And I speak Her words

She pumps my blood

And

She knits my bones.

I see Her in the eyes of my daughters

And in the faces of my Sisters.

Her presence invades my consciousness like perfume

With Her I give up the struggle for survival and I live.

She calls to me and I answer.

Around 5am, the following morning, I was woken by knocking on my window. When I opened the curtains, the raven was outside, knocking on the glass. Although that frightened me, I knew that I was being called by raven. I sat down, attuned, and felt a female energy. She was wearing a cloak which was a blueish, purplish, black colour. I could not see any of her features. For some reason, I could hear her breathing. It was almost as if I started to breathe her breath. It sounds odd, but that is how it felt.

A few days later, I was guiding a tour. My *anam cara* (soul friend) JulieMc was driving. One of the places we visited was a cave on Valentia Island. In the cave, I felt the feminine energy again and my breath started to feel strange. JulieMc had left the cave, as the energy was too much for her. The women and I went further in. Suddenly, we could hear lots of dogs barking outside. We continued to the back of the cave and, to the left, a stone was sticking out in the outline of a man's face. Next to and behind that stone, was a female face. This was the energy that had been calling me and I knew that this was raven.

When we came out, I asked JulieMc about the dogs.

"Amantha," she said, "it was the weirdest thing. These dogs came running towards the cave and, instead of going into the cave, they started climbing up the sides. It was very, very steep and they kept trying to climb up and they kept falling down and climbing up and falling down. There were about ten or twelve of them. I don't know where they came from or whose they were and then they were gone."

One of the women who was with us taught psychology in America and she said that some Greek or Roman goddess had dogs protecting her cave.

After that, I felt her with me all the time. When I tuned in, I got that purplish colour. I could see her outline and knew that she worked with magic.

When I moved back to Ireland, I met Eileen, a woman whom I have always seen as an elder. She had grown up near the bridge to Valentia. Eileen talked to the old people there and found the names, Mog Ruith and Tlachtga. As soon as Eileen said the name, it was as if the cloak opened and I knew her.

I could not find anything written down about them, so I journeyed and was shown Mog Ruith and Tlachtga. His stories were similar to the later stories associated with Merlin. Tlachtga was his daughter and he taught her everything.

When I go somewhere and begin to work with the energies, people become attracted to that place and go there. After I started that work, the energy began to be known. Whenever I talked about Tlachtga and Mog Ruith, I got more information about them. I saw her clearly with other priestesses. She was very much of her own energy. It was before Christianity and she and her father journeyed shamanically.

In the year 2000, my mother was diagnosed with cancer for the second time. The first time she had it, I had seen the cancer and a malignant polyp was removed in time. Twelve years later, I had no indication of her cancer before she was diagnosed. I brought her home to where I live, which is the place where she grew up. Her family had lived on the farm at the bottom of the hill below my house. Tlachtga was with me for this whole journey, so I knew that she was connected to death. When my mother was passing over, I knew that it was to Tlachtga she was going. After that, Tlachtga was always with me and there was no fear that, because she was with me, I must be dying. I was able to acknowledge her and that part of me that was connected to her. Even now, when I talk about her, I can feel her energy.

It is to Tlachtga I go when things are too difficult and I need to release them. If I am working with someone who is dying or someone who has passed over and is still tied to the earth's plane, Tlachtga assists me with that work.

When I first journeyed to Tlachtga, it was a very deep shamanic journey. All I could see was a shadow somewhere way before me with a small light behind her. It was not strong like sunlight, just a little light in the darkness. I was walking through a barren field with no grass or trees, but I kept tripping. After a while, I looked down and saw bones and skulls everywhere. I had been tripping over them. When I got to her, I felt as if I was moving from one place, one way of being into the next, almost like an initiation. It was also a releasing of something and a taking on of something else. Tlachtga put her hand into my body, pulled out my liver and gave it to me to eat. I had been a non-meat eater for years and had rarely eaten red meat. Eating a hot, dripping, raw liver was quite an initiation. I realised that it was also a releasing of something I was carrying and a taking on of something I was yet to fully understand.

Entrance gate to the Hill of Ward, Athboy, County Meath.

IMBOLC

The Goddess Brigit

From Samhain we move to Imbolc, the first day of spring, where the patroness is Brigit, the goddess of fertility and regeneration. (Brigid, Bridget, Brighid, Bride, Brid and Briget are different spellings of the name.) Brigit is a triple goddess, keeper of the hearth/fire, patroness of the arts/crafts and the midwife/healer.

Homage to Brigit goes back thousands of years. She was a prominent earth goddess of our ancient people in Ireland. As a triple goddess, Brigit had three different roles in one.

Brigit was a keeper of the flame. The fireplace is at the heart of the house. Without fire, people could die of cold or hunger during the winter months. Brigit was the keeper of the hearth, which in Irish is often called *neart* (strength or life force). *Neart* is also the heart. We see pictures of Jesus with a flame in the heart.

Fire belongs to the Lower World. In arcane teaching, we move the fire of passion from our base chakra into the heart where it becomes compassion. In old paintings, saints always had an aura or glow around their heads and that was the symbol for passion moving into compassion. Fire, for Brigit, is the heart fire as well as the hearth. A fire temple was built in Kildare in her honour. That flame was kept alight continuously for millennia until the Christians came and extinguished it.

She was also the midwife and healer. When we work with women giving birth, we call upon Brigit to assist us and have symbols of Brigit around us.

Brigit was the patroness of the arts. In the old days, the arts had to do with transformation – changing something into something else. Originally the arts were the ability to scry and to see (in the sense of being a seer). It was the cultivation of the third or inner eye, to see beyond and within. They included clairvoyance, divination and the ability to vision.

Another part of the arts was the ability to shapeshift and to move into different realms or realities. It had to do with opening. As patroness of the arts, Brigit not only transformed things around her but she transformed by what she brought through her.

Later on, the definition of the arts changed to become leathercraft, bread making, jewellery making and things of that nature and the visionary and journeying elements were lost.

Brigid, Nun and Saint

In the 5th Century AD, the first woman in Ireland to be professed as a nun in the Christian tradition was given the name Brigid. This was done to attract people into the new religion and to draw people's awareness and attention away from the earlier, pagan tradition.

It is said that the woman who became Brigid the nun was born on a threshold. Her mother was a Christian slave who was owned by a pagan chieftain and Brigid was his daughter. The mother was working in the fields when she went into labour. As they carried her into the *rath* (house), she fell down on the threshold, between the outside and the inside, and gave birth. This symbolised Brigid's position on the threshold between the pagan and Christian traditions. The name Brigid also means bridge. Brigid really was a bridge between the ancient and the new, between the Goddess Brigit and herself, the Christian saint. She encompassed both.

St Mel, the bishop who presided over her profession as a nun, also read over her the form for ordaining a bishop. This may not have been a mistake, because when he realised what had happened, he said, "What God has done no man can undo".

Brigid had a following of women and needed land to build her monastery. Taking some of her postulants with her, she went to Kildare. The local chieftain was a pagan. He lived on the Curragh, an area of Kildare where there are miles of flat land. A great celebration was going on. She went in with her women and asked him if he would give her land. He laughed at her, this Christian woman, and he said, "Throw down your *brat*, woman, and whatever the *brat* covers you can have".

They stepped outside and all the men came out laughing. Brigid took off her cloak, her *brat*, and threw it on the ground. It grew and grew. When it became twenty acres, the chieftain said, "Enough! Take what you want and be gone".

She took just enough land to have her monastery and garden. To everyone's surprise, Brigid chose the site of the ancient fire temple and rekindled the flame, which had been burning for centuries before that, in honour of the earth goddess, Brigit.

She built her abbey beside a giant oak tree, which gave Kildare its name (*Cill Dara,* the Church of the Oak) and she founded schools and hospitals.

She lived with her community of sisters. Being together as women gave them the strength to go out and care for others, to practise the arts, healing and midwifery and to cultivate food. She and her nuns fed the poor and hungry and gave away whatever riches were given to them. Brigid also acted as arbiter in disputes, bringing balance and common sense whenever one chieftain was in conflict with another.

It is said that Brigid had nineteen nuns. Every night one of them tended the fire and kept it lit so that it never went out. After Brigid died, her nuns always left the fire unattended on the twentieth night and called upon Brigid to keep the fire going. "Brigid, Brigid, Sacred Flame; Brigid, Brigid, in your name," is the call that the nuns use. The fire never went out.

All of Brigid's successors, as Abbess of the Brigidine Order, were bishops until the 1100s. They were among the most powerful and influential figures in Irish monastic life. It is said that the other bishops sat at their feet.

The early Christian Church in Ireland was a blend of Christianity and the pagan tradition. Rituals were held out of doors. Easter was celebrated on a fixed date; it was not a movable feast. Clerics were monks rather than priests and were allowed to marry, as were nuns. Women held positions of power within the church. Abbots and abbesses of the Celtic monasteries were often brothers or sisters of local chieftains. Women still took their mothers' names and owned land. Some women were chieftains.

Rome was thousands of miles away and seemed irrelevant to Irish Christians. Pope Adrian IV became concerned, particularly because women were refusing to pay taxes to the Roman church for land that they themselves owned. The Pope gave Henry II of England permission to intercede on his behalf, to bring the Irish church under the Roman system and reform governance and society throughout the island. As a result, all of the monks were told that they could either leave Ireland, leave their wives and children and become priests, or die. It also led to the Norman invasion of Ireland, so the whole story of Ireland and Christianity changed at that time. Women began to lose their power and their land. That happened in Ireland a lot later than in the rest of Europe. The traditions are still quite strong here.

In Kildare, Brigid's rekindled flame was kept burning for centuries, certainly until the twelfth century and possibly until the suppression of the monasteries in the sixteenth century, when Brigid's nuns are thought to have been killed. A twelfth century, Norman cathedral, built on the site, still stands today. All that remains of the earlier, monastic site is a round tower, a partial high cross and the remains of what is thought to be the fire temple.

The Brigidine Order was started again in 1807, in Tullow, County Carlow, by Bishop Daniel Delany. In 1992, the nuns returned to Kildare and in 1993 Sister Mary Teresa Cullen re-lit the fire of Brigid again. The flame was held in *Solas Bhríde* (Brigid's Light), their little house in Kildare town, and was tended by the Brigidine sisters there until the 1st of February 2006, when the (then) President of Ireland, Mary McAleese, accompanied by Sister Mary, carried the flame to the Market Square at the centre of Kildare town. A new sculpture had been commissioned and erected by Kildare County Council specifically to house Brigid's flame. It consists of a column with oak leaves above it and a fire cauldron in the shape of an acorn. (The oak leaves symbolise the Christian beliefs of St Brigid as well as the earlier, pagan worship of trees. They also represent Kildare – Brigid's Church of the Oak. The acorn, of course, is symbolic of new beginnings.) The cauldron was lit from the Brigidines' flame and burns perpetually in honour of Brigid.

On that occasion, President McAleese spoke about Brigid, Christianity and paganism, about the North of Ireland and the South and about taking all that was good from the past and carrying it forward. She said that we, like Brigid, need to be bridges.

When the Dalai Lama came to Ireland, he went to Kildare. There is a photograph of him and Sister Mary walking together holding hands, each carrying a Brigid's cross in their other hand. He really honoured the ancient feminine presence in Ireland.

The flame burns as a beacon of hope, justice and peace for Ireland and our world and is 'carried' by keepers of the flame in more than sixty-three countries. Women come in pilgrimage to the Brigidine Centre in Kildare to honour Brigid. There, they are welcomed by the wonderful women of the Brigidine Order, who personify the power of grace and humility.

Imbolc Traditions

People's homage to Brigid was so strong that, up until the 1920s, women often prayed to Brigid rather than Mary. She was called Mary of the Gaels. There was hardly a family in Ireland without somebody named Brigid. Many of the older churches had stained glass windows with pictures of Saint Brigid, Saint Columcille and Saint Patrick.

Many of our Imbolc traditions had to do with Brigit as keeper of the fire, the hearth, the home. Traditionally the fireplace was built first and the house was built around it. The hearth was the most important part of the cottage, because fire was essential: "Brigid keep the fire and Brigid keep the faith".

Fire kept the tribe together. Even up until the 1960s, when a house was built, the oldest woman of the family, (either the man's or the woman's), took hot turf from her fire, put it in her apron and carried it into the couple's new hearth where they built their fire around it. Then they kept that fire going. It symbolised the continuity of the tribe: the fire continued down through the family. Hearth fires were kept burning day and night before electricity was installed, which in some parts of rural Ireland was as recently as the 1950s or early 1960s.

When I was young, I remember the ritual when the old women cleaned out the fire. My granny did it too. Then they called on Brigid to keep the fire burning. Even in the 1940s and 1950s, when women spring cleaned their houses, they often walked around the house three times calling on Brigit to bless and protect the house. Brigit was also called upon in her role of midwife and healer. If a child was being born or someone was dying, they summoned her.

Imbolc was a time when people began to venture out of their homes and brave the weather after the winter. The cattle were brought out for short times of the day. It was a time when the waters and the wells were blessed. It is still a traditional belief that, if the weather is fine on Brigid's Day, we will have a good summer.

Brigid's crosses are made of reeds and are still used to protect the house. Traditionally, each family wove the crosses at home. Brigid's cross is hung over the doorway so that when people come in, they are blessed by Brigit. The blessing given by those who entered the house was:

Blessings to all in the house.

May you never know hunger and thirst.

Energy was also put into the Brigid's cross when it was being made:

May no harm or evil come into my house.

It is placed above the inside of the front door or sitting room door so that, if people come in and the intention they are carrying is not of light, it is released.

In recent times, a Brigid's cross is often hung like a crucifix, as the symbol of the Christian cross. Traditionally, it was hung in the shape of an X, representing the four main festivals of the Wheel: Samhain, Imbolc, Bealtaine and Lughnasa.

In Kerry where I live, especially around Kilgobnait, local people dress up in huge, conical, straw hats that hide their faces and they go from house to house on Brigid's Eve. They are known as the Biddies and they knock on doors, dance and sing. People bring them in and give them drink and food to carry forth. Nowadays, it is brought to the local community centre where the community gather to eat and drink together on Brigid's Day. Traditionally, the food and drink was given to those in need.

Opening the door at Imbolc is a ritual, allowing Brigit to enter, allowing the maiden to come into the house. The maiden brings laughter, light and delight. That is the tradition and nobody can tell you when it began. I spoke to an old man who said: "As long as I can remember, we've been doing it". It stopped for a while almost everywhere, but is being revived in Killorglin and elsewhere.

The symbols of Imbolc are water, fire and seeds. The colour is white, indicating the frost and snow upon the ground. It is also the white of milk. The udders of the ewes fill up with milk in preparation for the birth of their lambs. The new shoots of spring slowly awaken and break through the frost, snow and the hard earth.

A Personal Journey with Brigit

There was always an awareness of Brigit in my life. In my granny's house there was a big fireplace and we actually cooked over the fire. When Granny cleared out the hearth in the morning, she kept a little bit of turf to one side. Then she cleaned the fireplace, moved that hot turf back and built the new fire around it. She had a habit of throwing petrol on the fire. It often went whoosh and drops came out burning on the stone floor. She just put her foot on them and took no notice. Then she put the cauldron on the fire to cook.

Brigit as the midwife was always important. When one of my grandchildren was being born, we were unable to get the mother into the hospital in time. There was nobody else there, so I had to help her deliver the baby in the hospital car park. As the baby's head was coming out, I put my finger up and the cord was around its neck. So I called upon my granny and I called upon Brigit, as the midwife, to assist me. I put my finger in, pulled the cord very gently and it came down like a rope. When I did it, I knew exactly what I was doing. I was not nervous or in fear that I would kill, suffocate or strangle the child. I just did it, knowing on some level that I was doing it right. I felt I shapeshifted. I put the cord around the head and unwound it three times. As the baby was coming out, its face was going blue. I put my finger down the throat and blew into it. The baby slipped out on to my arms and started to cry a little. At this point a medic came and cut the cord and went running into the hospital with the baby.

They put my name as midwife on the certificate. I had never done that process before. Obviously, I knew about Brigit as the midwife because I called upon her at that time.

Around 1999, I met the Brigidine nuns in Kildare – Sister Mary and Sister Phil. They were such beautiful, kind women and for me they were the personification of Brigit. Whether you saw her as a saint or a goddess, they are the bridge between both, encompassing both and holding that space. I have the utmost love and respect for them, for the work that they do and for their kindness and grace. They have huge grace, yet they have huge passion and there is power in them. When I met them, they were holding the flame of Brigid in the house where they lived, in a council estate. They taught in the local school. I started visiting them and then bringing women there on pilgrimage. We had lunch and, afterwards, either Sister Mary or Sister Phil came with us to the fire temple and Brigid's wells, or to the labyrinth in the Curragh. They did sacred dance and angel cards and were not like any nuns I knew. At some point, Buddhist monks came and, with the nuns, put up a peace pole in the Curragh. It has Peace on Earth written in English and in ancient *ogham* script.

People see Brigit as the maiden, mother and crone in herself and that is true. Personally, I see Brigit more as the maiden, the place of beginnings. She holds that space. In my life, Mary has always been the Mother, because of Granny's beliefs. Brigit is somehow part of that energy, even though she is not the mother. She really is Mary of the Gaels.

Brigid's Well in Kildare town.

BEALTAINE

ꝼꞃⱷ Inꞵⷫc, ⱳⷷ ⷫⱷvⷷ ⱷ Bⷷⱥⱥⷫnⷷ.
30th April – 1st May, the first day of summer. The goddess who presides over Bealtaine is Medb, or Maeve, a great earth goddess, the keeper of the land. Homage to Medb goes back to ancient times, and originally, Medb was the earth goddess for all of Ireland, later being relegated just to Connacht.

Ireland had a matrifocal tradition, probably preceded by a matriarchy. For millennia, there was the tradition of the beanfeis (the sacred marriage). A priestess of the Goddess Medb was chosen and lay in Tara at a place called *Rath Medb* – a henge constructed in the third millennium BC. A chieftain was chosen for his wisdom, kindness and fairness to the people. He lay with the priestess of Medb on Bealtaine Eve and from their union came the fertility of the land and of the people. The priestess personified the Goddess Medb. She was the land. The chieftain was making love to, and giving his sperm to the land. Then he was head chieftain for that year.

This rite of passage went on until about AD 300-400, when Christianity came to Ireland. Brian Boru, the High King of Ireland, who lived at the end of the 900s and into the 1,000s, had a foot in both pagan and Christian camps and gave homage to Medb. When he became High King of Ireland, he followed the ancient rites. According to the oral tradition, he rode his horse through Blocc and Bluigne (two standing stones at Tara) which "leaned back both, to allow Brian Boru to ride through". He continued to follow the tradition for the inauguration at Tara. Each Bealtaine, he lay with a priestess of Medb at Tara and in this way he became the king of the people.

Queen Maeve and the *Táin**

The greatest epic we have in Ireland, the *Táin*, is about Maeve, Queen of Connacht, who came later than the Goddess Medb. In Sligo, there is a mountain called Knocknarea with a great cairn made of stones on top. It is called Maeve's grave and it is said that she is buried there, standing upright in her armour. That mountain can be seen from four counties: Sligo, Roscommon, Leitrim and Donegal. Medb holds that place and all of Connacht.

The story tells us that, for nine years in a row, Maeve chose Ailill to lie with her at the time of Bealtaine and to be the head chieftain. Obviously, she loved the man. One morning as they lay in bed, after some passionate lovemaking, Ailill turned to her and said, "I have a bull and my bull is the strongest and biggest bull in the whole land. Nothing and no one can come against my bull. So I no longer need you, Maeve, in order to rule this land."

"Are you mad, Ailill?" she replied. "You cannot take this land from me. For I am the land and the land is me." She promptly kicked him out of bed.

She found her son Fiachra and said to him, "I want you to go and look for the biggest, strongest and wildest bull in all the land. You must bring it back here and I don't care what you have to do to get it."

"Very well," he replied and off he went. He looked to the South, the East and the West, and he went to the North. In the North he found the small holding of a young chieftain of Cooley who had the largest bull he had ever seen – a huge, huge bull.

He went to the chieftain. "I am Fiachra, son of Maeve, and Maeve requests that we borrow your bull." The young chieftain was delighted. If she takes my bull, he thought, she might take me next. I might be head chieftain, why not?

* As Amantha's stories come from the ongoing oral tradition, rather than written versions, they have been adapted by storytellers through the generations. This version of the *Táin* features Fiachra, Maeve's son, rather than Ferdia, her warrior. It is set in Christian times and Cúchulainn has been converted to the new faith.

"Of course," he responded, "For Maeve, anything. I'd give my life for Maeve. Come, come we must celebrate."

They held a great feast and they sat and drank and they ate and drank some more. As they drank and drank, the soldiers of Maeve said to the young chieftain's soldiers, "Sure, if you hadn't given us that bull, we would have taken it by force!"

"You would not!" they retorted.

"We would," they said, "sure we heard Maeve telling Fiachra so."

Word went up to the chieftain. He looked at Fiachra. "Would you have taken my bull by force if I hadn't offered it to you?"

"Ah, don't worry," Fiachra replied. "Sure you offered us your bull."

"You must leave," commanded the chieftain. "And you cannot take my bull with you."

A huge fight ensued in which the chieftain was wounded. Fiachra and his men took the bull and began to travel, taking the brown bull of Cooley to Rathcroghan in Connacht, the royal seat of Maeve. The northern chieftain was bitter and angry. He called upon Cúchulainn to aid him and he told him his story.

Now Cúchulainn had grown up in the *rath* of Maeve – he was her foster son. Maeve had cared for him and loved him dearly. Fiachra was his foster brother and they loved each other as brothers. They had grown up together, learnt to fight together, learnt letters and poetry together and learnt how to woo young women together. Cúchulainn knew that Maeve had a wicked temper, but he had taken to the way of the cross and was a Christian. He felt this was an unchristian thing to do and that the land must be made anew in the name of Christianity. And he told the chieftain he would fight for him and would bring back his bull.

Cúchulainn amassed an army and followed Fiachra and his men. It is said that they met on the plains in an area we know now as Boyle. He met Fiachra in the field as the night was falling. It is a tradition in Ireland that one would never fight when the sun was not in the sky. So each went back to his own tent that night. As Cúchulainn lay sleeping Morrigan, the phantom queen associated with battle and death, appeared to him.

"Cúchulainn, lie with me, lie with me and let me carry your seed."

"Be gone with you and your pagan ways," replied Cúchulainn, "for I am now a man of the cross. Be gone from me."

The next day, Cúchulainn met Fiachra on the plains and they fought, each slightly hurting the other but neither wanting to kill or maim the other, for they were as brothers. That night, exhausted, they each went and lay to sleep. Again, as Cúchulainn lay on his pallet, Morrigan came.

"Cúchulainn, you will die in this battle, do not let your seeds go asunder. Let me carry them, let me carry them forth."

"Be gone with you and your pagan ways," he said. "Be gone!"

Cúchulainn and Fiachra went out fighting again the next day. This time, each of them was tired and angry. They gave each other cuts and little digs. By the evening, they were both bleeding profusely. Each of them was cleaned, washed and had his wounds sewn and each went to his bed. For the third and final night, Morrigan came.

"Cúchulainn," she said, "I beseech thee, I beg thee, please. You have left no seeds. You must lie with me." He turned away without a word.

On the third day, as he and Fiachra met again upon the plains, Morrigan flew as a crow, croaking over his head. Everyone knew that meant that he would die and, indeed that day, they both died in each other's arms.

The bull of Cooley was brought eventually to Maeve. When she heard, not just of her son's death, but also of the death of her foster son, she wept and wept and it is said that the whole of Ireland shook with her keening.

At last, her grief became anger. She sent her bull out against Ailill's bull and they fought and fought. They ran across the plains and through the trees fighting. They ran out on to the land, to the West, to the North and it is said that that battle goes on 'til this day, the battle between the sexes, between the matriarchy and the patriarchy. For the bull is synonymous with the male energy, taking the land. When Ailill had said to Maeve, "I do not need you any more to rule this land", he was taking in ownership what was being offered willingly to him, demanding what was being shared with him.

Bealtaine Traditions

Bealtaine is opposite Samhain on the Wheel and is, therefore, the balance of Samhain. Whereas Samhain brings us into the darkness and the ancestors, Bealtaine takes us out of the darkness, celebrating the light and the communion of the people with the land. It is important because the tribes come together to celebrate. The name Bealtaine is said to derive from Old Irish, meaning "bright fire".

Traditionally, at the time of Bealtaine, great fires were held and people travelled from all over to certain points on the landscape that were associated with Bealtaine. In Kerry, they met beneath the Paps, although the main Bealtaine fire was held at Uisneach, the centre, sometimes called the soul, of Ireland. The old people call it the bellybutton, as it is connected deep down into our Great Mother. It is the place of the essence of the feminine energy of Ireland, the triple energy of the maiden, mother and crone; it is the place of Éiru, the young maiden, and the *seanbhean,* the old woman, the ancient one, the Cailleach. Uisneach is not far from Mullingar. It is not a very high hill, but up to twenty counties are visible from there, on a clear day.

Until the late nineteenth century, a road connected Uisneach directly to Tara, the royal residence (where, of course, the *beanfeis* – the Sacred Marriage – took place at Bealtaine).

In Irish, County Meath is the Mide which is the fifth province of Ireland. We have four provinces in Ireland: Munster, Leinster, Ulster and Connacht. The fifth province, the Mide, contains the sacred Hill of Uisneach, the place betwixt and between. It holds the energy between here and the other realms.

Our stories tell us that, at the very centre of Ireland, on the Hill of Uisneach, there was a great fire temple where the fire never went out. On the eve of Bealtaine, all other fires in Ireland were extinguished. As the dawn rose on Bealtaine, runners took lights from that central flame at Uisneach and ran out across the land. Other runners came and met them and took lights from them and more runners came and took lights from them. By the night of Bealtaine, every fire in Ireland was lit from the one fire. Fire united the people. It was an important tradition, just as fostering was – you would not fight with your neighbour if they were caring for your child. In the same way, the Bealtaine fire united the people of the land because, where you have one fire, you have one people, one tribe.

Bealtaine was the time of coming together for merrymaking, love-making and great festivities. It is held by Medb and the Green Man. The tribes came from the four directions, Munster in the South, Ulster in the North, Connacht in the West and Leinster in the East. From the four sides, they climbed the steep hill, where the celebrations began after sunset on Bealtaine Eve. Festivities started in the night and went on into the day.

Couples came together at Bealtaine, to try the relationship out. At that time, women could choose their partners just as much as men could. If the relationship suited both, then they could have a hand-fasting ceremony at Lughnasa.

In our matrifocal tradition in Ireland, a woman could divorce her husband at any time, but a man could only divorce his wife at Bealtaine. Any children born from the woman's womb were full blood brother and sister, regardless of who the father was. Women carried the tradition. Children born of the same father, by different mothers, were half-brother or half-sister. The children conceived at Bealtaine were born at Imbolc and were considered sacred.

At Uisneach there is a stone called the Cat Stone with a hole underneath it. When deals were done at Bealtaine, they placed a long, tubular, musical instrument under the Cat Stone. They created the sound under the stone, until the hill resounded with the energy. That deal had to be honoured and kept on pain of death, because the earth herself had heard and accepted it.

As the Bealtaine fires died down, people ran their cattle through them to cleanse them of any impurities, so they would be healthy and fertile for the summer months. Tribespeople and couples also jumped over the fires.

In today's world, Bealtaine is called May Day. Even in the eighteenth and nineteenth centuries, maidens danced on May Day. In England and Europe, they had maypoles with long ribbons that intertwined as they danced. In Ireland people put clouties (pieces of material) on a hawthorn bush for good luck.

Bealtaine fires had been lit continuously for five thousand years. I was told by a man from Tarbert, in North Kerry, that the last Bealtaine fire was held there in 1940. In recent years, people have been reviving the tradition of the Bealtaine fires again.

Recently, the festival of Bealtaine has been invoked again on the Hill of Uisneach. A beautiful earth statue of the face of Ériu has been erected and a Festival of Fires is held there. In 2017, the President of Ireland, Michael D. Higgins, lit the Bealtaine fire on the Hill of Uisneach. The previous Irish leader to light the Uisneach ceremonial fire is thought to have been the High King, Ruaidrí Ua Conchobair (c. 1116 – 1198), almost a thousand years ago.

The colour of Bealtaine is red, the red of blood and of passion. When we celebrate Bealtaine with a group that includes men, it is also the place of the Green Man, a personification of the god Pan. Then the colour is green as well as red. Green is the colour of all the luxuriant growth at the end of spring and of the fertility of the land.

A Personal Journey with Medb

I separated from my husband and moved back to Ireland in 1997. Four months later, my ex-husband moved to Kerry. He was an American and had never lived in Ireland. Suddenly, he moved to Kerry to live with a woman who had been coming to me for shamanic healing. I felt violated. This place was my home and always had been. For him to move there, to the other side of the mountains from where I live, was very difficult for me.

I went to the Seven Sisters stone circle (what we call the grandmother's circle), outside Killarney, to ask for help. A woman appeared out of one of the stones. She looked like Xena (the warrior princess of the television series) but she was fair, whereas Xena was dark. She threw me a spear. I caught it. "Fight!" she said.

"What about forgiveness?"

"Fight first," she said, "forgive later."

That shifted me. It was just what I needed. Medb's warrior energy came into me. I needed her to inspire me to move from where I was, into where I needed to be. Then I thought, do I really want to be part of his drama, dharma, or karma anymore? And I thought, no I do not. I can just let go of it. Because Medb was an archetype, I was able to draw from that and to understand it. She really got me activated out of 'poor me what am I going to do?' into 'fuck this, I'm not accepting it!' She got my fire going again.

That was the time when Medb started stepping into my life. She helped me to regain my power again. My ex-husband never supported us financially or emotionally. When I moved back, I had glandular fever and the children and I had nothing. My two youngest were seven and nine and were solely dependent on me, because there was no one else. They had grown up in a community on the outskirts of London and were used to having lots of people around them. Suddenly, they were in a strange land, a strange school. I had to be very present for them as well as dealing with the break-up, being ill and trying to make money. The presence of Medb sustained me. I began to draw upon that energy.

I met Margot around that time as well. That woke up my passion, which had never really been woken by the men in my life. It had always been about their needs. I had become a kind of mother in a way, supporting them and taking care of them. Suddenly, I was embracing my wildness and passion and was finding that strength to get through things. That was Medb energy. Medb was very strong and a great support to me at that point, helping me to gather myself back together. She put a sword in my hand and she got me there.

Then in 1998, I was called by the ancient old woman of the land, to go to the centre of Ireland and, maths being my subject at school, I sat down and calculated the centre via latitude and longitude. We drove up from Kerry by car and managed to find a guest-house before dusk became night. The next morning, at breakfast, I saw a leaflet talking about Uisneach. My heart started racing and I knew this was the place She was calling me to.

There were no signs for Uisneach in those days so I found it by energies pulling me. We went through a field of young bullocks, through hedges and up the hill, the vibration getting stronger and stronger. Suddenly I was standing in front of the Cat Stone. When I put my hand upon it, I burst into tears, for here She was. She was Ériu, the maiden. She was Mother and she was the Cailleach. She was the land and this was/is Her doorway.

Information and ancient memories came flooding through me and as I spoke them, Margot was sitting beneath the stone, writing down what she could on the only bits of paper we had, which happened to be a toilet roll. The rain was lashing and winds were blowing and my tears mingled with it all.

Afterwards we found the nearest pub and had a hot port each. There were two elder men there, slowly sipping at their Guinness by the bar and we engaged them in conversation. We asked about the hill we had just come from and about 89% of what I saw and channelled was what they shared with us on that rainy afternoon.

The face of Ériu sculpture on the Hill of Uisneach, County Westmeath.
Sculpture by Patsy Preston.

Goddess Tailtiú

Lughnasa, July 31st – August 1st, is held by Tailtiú, the gentle mother and by Lugh, the sun god. It is the place of the harvest.

Tailtiú is a very ancient goddess, a presiding presence over Tara. Some people call her Tea. She was the goddess of the Firbolgs, the giant race who lived in Ireland before the Tuath Dé. It is said that Tailtiú brought agriculture to Ireland, cleared the first plains, planted the first seeds and brought the first harvest. That tells us that, in the story of Ireland, it was the time when we were moving from hunter gathering and becoming agriculturalists.

In the story of our land, the Firbolgs were already here when the Tuath Dé arrived. At first, the two peoples got on well together, until a king of the Firbolgs became jealous of the Tuath Dé and started a battle. As he was dying, he said that he would regret it to the end of his soul's life.

Tailtiú lived at Tara and was renowned for her kindness and gentleness, but she died from her labours, so relentless was she in her cultivating and harvesting of the land. In the story, as I heard it in Kerry, Lugh was the sun god, son of the Dagda (the father god of the Tuath Dé) and Anu the mother goddess. They chose to give their son Lugh to Tailtiú to foster. That kept peace, to begin with, between the Tuath Dé and the Firbolgs. Tailtiú breastfed Lugh, cared for him and loved him.

So beloved was Tailtiú by Lugh that he started great games in her honour, in a place originally called Tailtiú but now called Teltown in County Meath, not far from Kells. Those great games were held around eight or nine hundred years before the Olympic Games began in Greece. People came from far and wide to compete: to see who could run fastest, throw furthest, jump highest, or whose horses were strongest. It is exciting that, now, in Ireland, archaeologists are beginning to prove our stories. They have found artefacts in Teltown that prove that games were held there.

Lughnasa Traditions

Lughnasa was a time of celebration for the harvest. Traditionally, the first bread was cooked from the new barley, rye and wheat and was given away. People received a gift of bread in return. The first apples were collected at this time and dipped in honey. Alcoholic drinks like cider and mead were made from grains, apples and honey. These were shared as part of the festivities.

It was also a time of handfasting ceremonies for couples who had come together at Bealtaine and chose to stay together – until the next Bealtaine at least!

Rather than marriage, as we know it today, they had handfasting. There was a big stone with a hole in the middle. For those young people who wanted to be with somebody but were too shy to ask, they had the boys dancing on one side blindfolded and the girls dancing on the other side, going in different directions. When the music stopped, they touched somebody on the shoulder and they had to put their hand out through the stone. When they touched their hand through the stone they were handfasted. Then they could see if they suited each other.

People gathered for great fires across the land, on specific hilltops, to celebrate Lughnasa. Lughnasa is represented by the colour gold, the colour of the harvested grains.

A Personal Journey with Tailtiú

I began to do pilgrimages (sacred journeys on the land) in Ireland in 1995. At first, the journeys were only in Kerry, then in Munster and then they expanded to include places throughout the whole of Ireland. Around the year 2000, we started going to Tara. There, I felt the presence of a very open, grace-filled, mother energy that still held the land there. I asked Michael, the man in the shop at Tara, about the energy and he said it was "Tea". That name did not feel right for me; it was not the name that was coming to me. So, I journeyed with her and she showed herself to me and showed me a beautiful mound where she was buried, in a place called Teltown. I am not sure whether the name came to me then, or whether somebody gave me the name Tailtiú.

I constantly talked about Teltown and people told me that there was no such place. But I knew she was not wrong. Why would she give me the name if it was not there? Tailtiú was really holding this space, holding and caring for the land and helping things to grow. She was supporting me in my work, helping people to be fed by the land of Ireland. When I brought the women out on pilgrimage, they were fed and could feel her energy.

As women it is easy to fall into the role of mother, whether we have children or not. We have a huge ability to create nourishment and to hold for others. Tailtiú was there, doing that for me and for the women on the tours.

Years later, I got a call from a woman who introduced herself as Renee who lived in Teltown House! "I heard about you. You know about Teltown!"

So, I visited Renee and her husband, Bartle, in Teltown House, near Kells. They are a beautiful couple and Renee epitomises the energy of Tailtiú in her generosity and kindness. I have been to the mound of Tailtiú, opposite the church in the townland of Teltown. Tailtiú was right: she was there.

Tailtiú showed me that place, how she breastfed her foster-son, Lugh and how she cultivated the land. When I got to know her deeply, I realised more and more that she is part of the living land, a face of the Mother. Each of the deities can be a triple goddess in themselves, encompassing the maiden, mother and crone. Tailtiú is part of that.

My parents were the hardest working people I ever met in my life, even to this day. But from when I was nine years old, I mothered my mother who became ill. When she came home from hospital, she spent quite a while in bed. So, I was cooking meals, going down to the shops and carrying the groceries home. My brother did not do it. My dad helped, but he was working too.

I never stepped back out of that role. By the time I was fifteen or sixteen, I was telling her what we were eating that night. I felt a loss, because it was I, rather than she, who took that role, but when she was ill, none of that was important. Later, it was Tailtiú who really mothered me, and I realised that I could be held by her.

Amantha at the Fairy Trees, Hill of Tara, County Meath.

SPRING EQUINOX

East, Boann

Tbere is an interval of approximately six weeks between each of the festivals of the Wheel calendar. Between Imbolc and Bealtaine is the East, the spring equinox, March 21st. At that time, night and day are in equal balance. It is said that if you get a fresh, raw egg (that has not been in the fridge), rub the flattened end on your clothes and put it on the countertop, it will stand up on its own because of the magnetic pull of the earth at that point.

The East is the place of Boann, our great river goddess. It is said that she was the most ancient of ancients, so little is known of her beginnings. When the earth was moving from molten rock, liquid and gas, into solid form, it is said that Boann brought waters from the Milky Way down through her breasts. The land was dry and parched and the milk that flowed from her breasts became the great River Boyne which was called after her. *Bó* in Irish means cow, so some see her as a cow goddess.

The River Boyne surrounds an area called Brú na Bóinne (the palace or mansion of the Boyne) which contains three megalithic cairns: Newgrange, Knowth and Dowth. These are some of the oldest engineered buildings in the world, built over a period of four hundred years, between 3330 BC and 2800 BC.

Newgrange is connected to the winter solstice: the light comes through the opening and enters the central cavity on December 21st. Dowth and Knowth are connected to the equinoxes. Newgrange has had restoration work on the outside, which was disturbed by peoples over the centuries, to return it to how they imagine it looked, whereas Knowth and Dowth have been relatively untouched. All three cairns are mathematically structured using greywacke stones that are ten to fifteen feet in length and five or six feet in width. The dark granite is warm on the coldest day, while the white quartz is cold on the warmest day.

In recent excavations, they discovered that the hieroglyphs (of which the triple spiral is the most famous), visible on the outside, are also on the backs of the stones. The ancient people built them knowing that nobody would ever see that artwork.

Entering the cairn at Newgrange, we go through a passage into a chamber. It is like going into the womb, the tomb of the mother. There are three smaller chambers, two of which are like ovaries. The tombs have been disturbed over the centuries, but usually contained cremated remains.

Knowth has what are called satellites, nineteen tiny cairns around the main cairn. They are also aligned with the movements of the sun and with the equinoxes and solstices.

Part of the power of Brú na Bóinne is the River Boyne surrounding it – Boann holding it sacred. At the time it was built, the planet was going through the age of Taurus, when the cow (rather than the bull) was worshipped. Many threads connect together here in the place of Boann.

The spring equinox is also the place of Manannán Mac Lir, the god of the sea who is said to be Boann's consort. The Isle of Man is called after him.

Manannán was just one of Boann's consorts, along with Elcmar and, some say, Neachtain.

The story is that the Dagda saw Boann and was drawn to her. He wanted to lie with her although she was already with Elcmar. The Dagda sent Elcmar away on an errand and, while he was gone, he stopped the sun and they lay together. He stopped the sun for the whole nine months until Boann had the baby – Aengus, the god of love – so that her husband would not know.

When Aengus was old enough, he knew that the Dagda was his

father and asked if he could stay in Newgrange for a day and a night. Aengus played the game back on his father. He stopped the sun and declared, "All there is is day and night, so now I take ownership of Newgrange".

Spring Equinox Traditions

The spring equinox is the first equal balance of light and dark in the year. We are moving from Imbolc towards Bealtaine. This balance gives us the opportunity to release all that we held in the winter months and to open ourselves to the incoming light. We start to feel a lightness in our steps. The sap that awoke at Imbolc begins to rise, as nature opens up her bounty around us. Buds grow and leaves unfold themselves again, often starting with the chestnut tree here in Ireland. Grass becomes greener. Fowls, calves and more lambs are born. The time of hibernation is complete, young animals frolic and we enjoy life all around us in nature. Flowers blossom – often starting with the daffodils which arrive early, with a promise of the sun yet to shine, bestowing its blessings upon us. Bees begin their flight and birds sing the earth awake again. It is a time of cleaning out after the winter, in body, mind and spirit as well as in the home. Often, the old folk did not take off their inner vests throughout the winter months, until spring, when they had their first full bath, sometimes in a tin bath, in front of the fire. The water was not wasted, as they then washed the clothes and sheets to hang out in the spring sunshine.

Many families ventured further afield at this time and some went on pilgrimage to a sacred glen or well, to be blessed on this day of equal light and dark.

The Irish hare, which is larger than the rabbit and has long ears, is connected to the spring equinox and is one of the symbols of the Goddess and fertility. It attunes with the full moon and is nocturnal. On spring evenings, it is often seen in its mating ritual, jumping up on its strong back legs, with its front paws forward, as if it is boxing. It is said that hares sit in circle under the full moon and this has given them a mystical quality. Many believed the hare was a shapeshifter and could change sex, linking it to the balance of the sun and moon, as well as identity. Its colour changes to grey in winter and back to brown in spring. For this reason, it is often connected with the Cailleach. Hares can bring illumination and the promise of balance. Traditionally, people carried a hare's foot, as a lucky charm, to guard against the illnesses of the day.

The tradition of the egg at Easter goes back way before Christianity, the egg being a symbol of fertility and the promise of birth. Hens begin laying more eggs at this time and farm people buy new hens. The ancient people usually killed a cow at the time and the blood was given to the land.

The colour of the spring equinox can be the blue, translucent colour of the river, or it can be pink, between the white of Imbolc and the red of Bealtaine.

A Personal Journey with Boann

When I was breastfeeding my third child, I could have fed three or four children. Once, when I lay in the bath, the water turned white with milk from my breasts. I thought, my god, the Milky Way! It seemed so powerful.

Boann started coming to me at that point. I did not know who she was, but I got that feeling of the Milky Way and she showered me with white crystals. She showed me stars and gases. It was like a sudden bang, a convergence of something, then things started to solidify. As that happened, she brought the Milky Way down through her. It flowed out of her breasts and flowed as a river on to the land of Ireland. The movement of it flowing through her breasts was like a song. It was like hearing the wind but, it was the water which had its own song. As it flowed onto the land its song seemed to wrap, somehow, around the land and become part of it. The song was also the dream and the dream was singing itself on to the land, through the water. Later, people who drank from it could dream and sing and their sounds became part of the land too. By drinking the waters, we were an extension of the land. Boann brought water and also brought the dream. That is why she is in the place where we dream, the place of the young girl, the dreamer.

We know that our body is made up of sixty percent water. My brother Thomas and I used to go across the field at Granny's to get fresh spring water. When we grow up drinking water from where we live, we take in the elements of what is there: calcium, magnesium, or whatever is in the waters. By taking in those minerals, we become part of that place.

Entrance to Newgrange cairn at Brú na Bóinne, County Meath.

SUMMER SOLSTICE

South, Áine

The goddess of the summer solstice, the 21st of June, is Áine. She is also the fairy queen. Áine holds Lough Gur in County Limerick, a place of continuous human habitation for at least six thousand years. In front of Lough Gur is the Grange stone circle, the largest stone circle in Ireland, with over one hundred and thirty-three stones. From the 20th to the 23rd of June, if the morning is clear, the rising midsummer sun shines right into the centre of the stone circle. I have been there on many solstices and it has only been clear twice.

At the summer solstice, the veil is thinnest between our world and the fairy realms. We can get in touch with the fairy folk, elementals or nature spirits then, more than at any other time. There is magic in the air at the summer solstice.

In between the flowering at Bealtaine and the harvest at Lughnasa, the fruit grows through the summer. Áine's fire impregnates the germ of life into the fruit that will become our harvest. She brings fire and inspiration and awakens the life force within us too.

As long as people can remember, the locals walked around Cnoc Áine (Áine's Hill), on the 20th of June, carrying lights and calling upon Áine to bring in the sun. They needed the sun to grow their grains and for a good harvest. The land needed to be dry for a while for their potatoes and vegetables to grow. People called on Áine to bring the life force to their fields, to themselves and to their stock.

Áine is also seen as a triple goddess. The other two aspects of Áine are the old woman and the mermaid, both of which are associated with Lough Gur. Nobody quite understands the connection with the mermaid. The local story is that, if you go deep down into that lake, you can go through a channel into the sea. I do not know if that is a fact, because I could not hold my breath for that long! However, they have found seashells at Lough Gur. At first, they thought they might have been dropped by seagulls, but there were too many for that.

There are several stories associated with Áine. In the middle of the nineteenth century, around 1856-7, British soldiers were garrisoned all around Ireland. There was a curfew in place and no Irish people were allowed out after 9pm. The people from the Cnoc Áine area asked the local captain if they could walk around the hill on Midsummer's Eve, as that was their tradition. They were refused permission. It is actually recorded in the garrison's notes that, coming up to midnight on that night, a lone woman, cloaked and hooded, walked around the hill carrying a light and that the soldiers were too frightened to approach her. From that time onwards, the captain allowed them to be out after midnight on that one night of the year. The locals, to this day, will tell you that that was Áine. Because, from time immemorial, they had walked for her, on that night she walked for them.

Summer Solstice Traditions

The summer solstice is the longest day of light in the year in the Northern Hemisphere. It celebrates the regenerative, life-giving sun. On that day, our souls vibrate with the source of light of the sun and rise up, to open to the expansion of light – even though we might not be aware of it. Bonfires are held in many places around the world, reflecting the light back to one of our main sources of life, outside of this living earth.

Throughout Ireland, great bonfires were lit on the eve of the summer solstice and blessings were sent to the crops. It was the mid-point between Bealtaine and the harvest. People gathered to sing, eat, drink and make merry. Often, as the fire began to die down, people jumped over it for good luck. Old crops and destructive weeds were burnt, to make way for new growth. The oak becomes the king of the forest, taking over from the holly of winter. Wheels made of dry wood were set on fire to roll down the hill, as a symbol of the sun which, after this night, begins its slow descent into darkness again.

There was a time when parents would not allow their children under the age of three to go outside on the summer solstice. They kept them in the house with the door locked because they were frightened that the fairy folk would take them and leave a fairy changeling in their place. If their child became wilful, they would think they had a changeling. What happened to that lovely docile child? The fairies must have taken him or her. So, they hid their children at the solstice. In some areas they used dandelions or foxgloves to keep the fairies away.

Fire is the element of the summer solstice. The colour is amber, between the red of Bealtaine and the gold of the harvest. It is also flame-coloured – the blending of red and gold.

A Personal Journey with Áine

I first met Áine when I went to Lough Gur and the Grange stone circle, after I moved back to Ireland. The Grange stone circle is dedicated to Áine and, although I knew of Áine before that, I had never been there. As a group, we went to the stone circle for the solstice sunrise. When the sun rises, it shines into the centre of the circle. I felt the fire and inspiration that it brought and felt myself awakening. It was delightful. I felt fully awake within myself.

In my youth I had been a hippie and loved going to festivals and sitting around the fire at night with everybody singing and sharing food. It was part of my being, because my family came together for birthdays, weddings, communions and funerals and sang together and shared food. Being a hippie was like an extension of that for me, but I did not have the opportunity to indulge that part of myself for long, as I married at twenty and was a mother at twenty-two.

I never had much time being that wild, rainbow woman, because I had married so young. When I came back to Ireland, I started embracing that side of myself and gradually letting that come through. Áine inspired me to bring that forth. I was in a relationship with a woman and, around where I lived, no other women were in a relationship together. Part of me began to accept that I was not like other people. Rather than trying to fit in any longer, I decided to be who I am. Maybe I had always been like that, but I did it consciously then.

It was difficult because we were living in a rural area which was conservatively Catholic at the time. My son, especially, did not want his friends to find out about my relationship. On one side, I had to contain that for my children, while on the other, I allowed myself to live in the fullness of my nature. I was also trying to let them know that it was not wrong. Yet, I was doing what they wanted, hiding it, so that I could keep them safe. Áine really inspired me through that.

Moving to the countryside, I became very aware of the changing seasons. When June comes and we have seen the lambs, calves and foals of Bealtaine, Áine then brings the life force into the fruit that we will eat. The barley and the hay ripen through her. She became more present in my life because of that.

Amantha at entrance stones to Grange Stone Circle, County Limerick.

AUTUMN EQUINOX

West, Macha

CDACDA IS CDE ᵍODDESS/ARCDETYPE CUDO DOLOS CDE
autumn equinox (September 21st) in the West. She is an ancient
horse goddess and shapeshifter. In our stories of Ireland every mythic
people who came to Ireland had a Macha with them. So we know
that Macha was a title, rather than an individual person. It was a
position held by a woman. The Firbolg were the people who lived in
Ireland before the Tuath Dé and, before them, we had the Nemods.
The very first Macha was a goddess of the Nemods, so she was a very
ancient goddess. Little, if anything, is known of the first Macha.

The next Macha we come across is one of the Tuath Dé. This Macha came, it is said, to Cruinniuc who was a minor chieftain. One
evening, as he was riding back from hunting with his two young
sons, there was a small woman standing outside his *rath*. She was
cloaked and hooded and he could not see her face.

When they reached the rath, she stepped forward and put her hand
upon his horse. He was afraid that the horse would go for her because
it was a wild horse and, normally, would only be calm for him. As she
put her hand out, the horse put his head down and neighed beside
her. The woman looked up at Cruinniuc and he found himself looking into two, big, beautiful, brown eyes in a small heart-shaped face.
She was a tiny woman, standing there looking at him. For a moment
he could say nothing. He got off the horse and, before he could utter
a word, she had taken the horse around the side of the *rath*. As he
watched, she walked around the *rath* three times, blessing the *rath*
and invoking the energies of the ancient ones – the Tuath Dé.

Then she stepped inside and he and his sons stepped in behind her. They could smell beautiful broth and there was fresh bread on the table. She fed them and gave them drink and spoke not a word. That night, when he went to bed, she came and lay beside him. She told him that her name was Macha and she had been watching him. She had seen how he was with his two sons, his love for them and his kindness and gentleness towards them and she had fallen in love with this man. The chieftain had been alone for many years. His wife had died in childbirth. He grew to love this woman. His sons loved her too. Each day, they would go hunting and sometimes she would go with them. She wouldn't take a horse; she would run beside them and, even when the horses were tired, she could keep running. He had never seen anyone run the way she ran.

Time moved, as time does, and Macha became pregnant. The chieftain felt his heart would burst with pride and love. It filled him with great joy to think that he would hear the sound of a child again in the *rath* and he would hold this tiny body beside him.

It came to the time of the great games. He felt that it was time his sons came with him to meet other chieftains' sons and perhaps their daughters too. They were growing up. As well, he had a secret ambition. That was to win a prize for his Macha. He hoped to bring back a semi-precious stone, to let her know how much he loved her.

To his surprise, she wasn't happy at all at the idea of him going to the games. She begged him not to go. He thought this was just the pregnancy and that she was worrying unnecessarily. No matter what she said, he was determined to go and to take his sons. As they got ready to leave and he was getting up on his horse, she came out and she said to him, "You must promise me that you will tell no-one that I am here. Tell not who I am, where I come from, nor what I can do. You must promise me."

He laid his big hand upon her very small little hand. "Do not worry, my love," he said. "Do not concern yourself. I will say not a word." And kissing her on the brow, he was gone with his two boys.

It was evening by the time they reached Teltown. A great assembly had already gathered, tents had been put up, branches of trees had been bent over, blankets had been thrown upon them and skins to keep the people warm at night. Fires were lit already. Excitement was in the air. He sent his sons off to meet others. He went to bed for he was going to go into the running race and the jump and the stone throw. He had put himself down for almost everything, so desperate was he to bring at least one prize back to Macha.

The next day, when the games began, he came second or third in every competition and he won nothing. At the end of that day he felt frustrated, ashamed and embarrassed. He heard some young men laughing. He looked up at them and, misconstruing it, he said to them, "Ha! You're laughing at me? You're laughing at me because I haven't won anything. You can laugh away, because I have a woman called Macha and she can run faster than even the great chieftain's horses."

They looked at him in shock, because they hadn't even been talking about him. And then he realised that they weren't looking at him, they were looking behind him. There was silence and he turned around. There, standing behind him, was Mac Neasa, the High King. He looked back at the chieftain and he said, "You have a woman? What did you call her? Macha? And she can run faster than my horses?" Ah, too late, too late, he realised what he had done.

"Ach no, no my liege," he said. "I spoke in haste. I spoke in anger. Sure, she's only a local girl, you know."

"She can run faster than my horses?" The High King replied, "I want to see this woman. Bring her here now."

"Oh, my liege, she cannot journey now because she is heavy with child!" The king waved him away. Then he told the soldiers to take him and bind him and he sent them out to the chieftain's *rath*.

Macha was sitting by the fire when she heard the sound of many horses and her heart was heavy like lead. She was finding it hard to breathe, for she knew something had gone terribly wrong. Next, there was banging on the door. She pulled herself up, holding her belly, and she went over and answered the door. Standing there were the soldiers of the High King.

"Are you Macha?"

"Yes," she said, holding herself up.

"The High King demands that you come now."

"Sure, I can't come now. Look at me. I am heavy with child."

"Well," the soldier said, "if you do not, woman, then your husband is dead." And so Macha knew she had to go.

So she stepped out and they lifted her up, like she was a feather, and placed her upon a horse. And she had to journey through the night. Every movement of the horse was like daggers sticking in deep inside her. When she arrived at the great assembly, she was exhausted. She was pale white. They lifted her down and her knees were going from under her.

The High King looked down at this little woman who was heavily pregnant. This man is mad, he thought. I'll show them all how stupid he is.

"Well," he said, "I hear that your name is Macha and that you can run faster than my horses."

"Aw, no," she said, falling to her knees. "No, no, no, my liege. Sure, I cannot run at all. I am heavy. Heavy with child."

"Well, woman," he said, "run you will. Otherwise, you will never see your husband again."

They got four of the High King's fastest horses and they tied them together and brought Macha to the starting line. She took her *brat* from her shoulders and tied it tightly around her to hold her belly up. She stood there and, when they dropped the stone, she ran and the horses ran and, indeed she did run faster than the King's horses. Macha ran across the finishing line before the horses but, as she did, she fell down deep in the throes of labour. There in front of the startled crowd she gave birth to twin boys. As she did, she felt her life's blood pouring out of her. She put her hand down into her blood and threw it towards the High King and his men. "You come from Ulster and I will curse you with the birth pangs of labour. And I will curse you and all those who come after you that you will never know peace." And with that she died. It is said that that curse is still there today and that there will never be peace.

The second Macha story was five or six hundred years later. She was the daughter of a chieftain called Áed Rúad and she was his only child. He had given her the name Macha to bring her strength, for her mother had died in labour. Her mother had been one of the shining ones, one of the *sidhe,* the Tuath Dé. Her father had asked for another of that lineage to come and care for her as she grew. And so, this Macha was brought up with the stories of her people, of her mother's clan. As her father grew older, he trained Macha so that she could be chieftain after him. He taught her how to care for the people, what to do with the animals and how to protect the *rath.*

A time came when he grew very ill. It was such an illness that his skin began to peel off him. There was a terrible smell. It was so bad that people could not go near him. Each day Macha, who loved her father dearly, would go in and wash him, change the cloth around him and she would sit with him and talk to him. As it came near to his death, her father's brother came to see him. He had taken to the new ways, to the way of the cross, and he brought with him two men of the cloth. "Macha," he said, "I have come to see my brother and I have brought these men to bless him in the Christian ways."

Macha looked at him. She knew her father would never take to these new ways. "Of course you can see him, Uncle," she said. "For you are of his blood. But you must call me before he dies."

"Ah, worry not, Macha," he said, patting her. "I will call you of course." And he went in with these two and closed the door upon her. He was there an hour, then two hours. When the doors opened, he came out holding a parchment and he said to her, "Macha, your father has gone. He has been blessed in the Christian faith and he has signed this to say that I would take the land and rule here."

She looked at him and said, "That's not possible. My father would never sign that. He wasn't even healthy enough to lift a hand. This land is my land. These people are my people."

"I'll tell you what I will do," he replied. "We will marry so that you too can stay with me and we will rule together."

She took a step back and she said, "Uncle, I cannot marry you!" Oh my goodness, she thought to herself, this dirty old man.

"No, no," he said, "we will not join in union physically, but we will rule together."

No matter what she said, with this parchment in his hand she felt that there was little she could do. Before her father's body was even cold, the two of them were married. He was thinking he'd get rid of her soon enough. But halfway through the wedding feast, he became ill and died. Some said it was wild celery, but nobody was sure what caused it.

That day he'd sent for his three sons, to call them back to Ulster, so that they could now be princes. And these three sons were delighted with themselves. They travelled back and, as they did, they heard word that their father had died and they knew that Macha had something to do with it. She knew about potions and things that they didn't. So they began to amass an army. The night before they reached her, they sent the army out to find food and to take what they wanted.

The three lads sat around the fire talking about all the riches and the women they would have and discussing which one of them would be the chieftain, seeing as their father had died. They were sitting there talking and laughing and drinking. Suddenly, this old woman came out of the trees towards the fire. She was toothless and smelly and hairy.

"For God's sake, get her out of here!" So the younger one got up and walked ahead of her. He walked into the woods and she hobbled behind cackling.

As she walked into the woods she changed back into Macha. The stone that she had inside her *brat* came out and, as he turned towards her, she hit him on the head. He fell down. She tied him up to a tree and gagged him. She left him there and, walking back, she shape-shifted into a beautiful young woman with her buxom breasts half coming out of her bodice. She walked towards the fire. The two boys were pushing each other back.

"Ha ha, lads," she said, "I can take you both, but one at a time." The one who was throwing the other one down, ran into the woods behind her, and she laughing. She ran around a tree. He ran around behind her and, bang, she hit him on the head, tied him to the tree and left him gagged beside his brother. Then she waited a little time, but only a little because he was young.

She went back again. "Are you ready?" she said to the third.

"I am I am," he said, jumping up and beginning to unlace his pants already. She ran into the woods again with him behind her. She turned and she hit him on the head and knocked him out. She tied him up and gagged him beside his brothers. Coming back into her own being, she stood leaning against another tree and waited.

Night passed, dawn came. The boys began to awaken. She was sitting there watching and, when they saw her, realisation began to dawn upon them.

"Ha!" she said. "You thought you could come and take my land. You thought you could just walk in here with an army. You thought I wouldn't be told, that my people wouldn't tell me. Listen carefully, you have two options. You can either be killed right now, or you can build me the biggest *rath* this land has ever seen. And after you have built this *rath* you will leave by boat and you will never return."

The three of them looked at her. Did she think they were going to do this? They were pulling at the ropes. They couldn't get away. Gradually they realised that there was nothing they could do.

"Well, lads," she said, "what's your answer?" The young men knew they had been bested. They could do nothing but agree.

They built a *rath* that was known as the biggest, largest *rath* in Ireland. It was built on the mound called Eamain Macha (sometimes translated as Macha's Twins), now called Navan Fort in Armagh (Ard Mhacha – Macha's Height). Recently, archaeologists have found that there was once a ceremonial enclosure there, the biggest in Ireland.

Both stories of Macha touch us deeply and give us an opportunity to see certain aspects of ourselves. For that reason, Macha is associated with the cave of becoming and undoing (which we discuss later in Walking the Wheel). The first Macha story is one of undoing. She suffered and was abused because she asked for silence that was not kept and so she died. The second is a story of becoming, where she used plant medicine and shapeshifting to overcome the enemies who plotted against her. She fought for her land and what was hers. In her role as protector of the land, she was the mother.

Autumn Equinox Traditions

The autumn equinox is the second day of the year when day and night are in equal balance. This day reminds us of what is ahead, in the great turning of the Wheel, as our days of sun will get shorter and shorter. The leaves are turning gold, red and brown and beginning to drop down from where their life started, onto and into the living earth. Rich acorns and hazelnuts also drop and can be used to plant or to eat. It is the time of the second harvest. Turf that was cut in early summer is, hopefully, dry and light in weight now and is being collected and brought in from the bog-fields for use in household fires. People begin to focus on their homes now, making them ready for storms and, perhaps, snow. It is a time when we become aware of turning slowly inwards, moving into a place of rest and reflection.

All of the crops should have been brought in now and we make preparation for storing them safely throughout the winter. There are places in Ireland where we can still see the remains of stone sweat lodges, which were often used at the time of the autumn equinox, to cleanse people and keep them healthy, before they moved into the winter months.

The colour of the autumn equinox is brown, the earthy colour of the cave. It is between the gold of Lughnasa and the black of Samhain.

A Personal Journey with Macha

I do not remember when I met Macha, if somebody told me the story, if I read it, or if I heard it around the fireplace with Granny and her friends.

There was a period in my life when Macha was there. I had the feeling that I could not do all that I wanted to do. I had to hold myself back. I wanted to run, I wanted to go, but I had to hold in and hold back. So I must have known the story of Macha, at that stage, and how she had died racing.

The second story of Macha came to me later. Somebody told me that story and I found myself journeying with it. As I did, I kept hearing, "Every people that came to Ireland had a Macha with them." And I knew that she was letting me know that she had always been here.

At the time that Macha came to me, I really wanted to go to Eamain Macha in Armagh. Margot and I went there and climbed to the top of the mound. Macha's energy was so strong, as if she was telling me that the cave was inside the mound. "This is my cave. This is where I am. This is what I hold."

Eamain Macha, Navan Fort, County Armagh.

WINTER SOLSTICE

North, The Cailleach

The last point on the eightfold wheel is the winter solstice, December 21st, in the North. It is the place of the Cailleach, the old woman, hag, crone, wise and ancient one. The Cailleach is much revered in our tradition. She holds the stories and the memories. In Patrick Pearse's famous poem, Ireland herself is seen as the old woman, the *seanbhean*.

"Mise Éire.

Sine mé ná an Chailleach Béara."

(I am Ireland. Older am I than the Hag of Beara.)

The North is also the place of the grandmothers. In our tradition and many traditions around the world, the grandmothers held the stories and wisdom of their people and carried them forward. They could hold space and had time available to them. The grandmothers told the stories to the young ones while the mothers cooked, hunted, wove or turned the land. In those tribal traditions they held great stories and great ways of knowing and being.

Every one of us has grandmothers. I do not just mean our mother's or father's mothers, but all the women who have walked before us who now hold space for us. We stand on their shoulders.

We are in the process of reclaiming the stories of our grandmothers. I was very blessed to have a grandmother who told me the stories which fed me more than anything else in my life. They became part of my weave. The stories hold and revive us and remind us of who we are. Traditionally people took care of the grandmothers and grandfathers. Up to fifty years ago, a grandchild sometimes went to live with one when the other had died. How do we care for them now? Many have passed on without their stories being told.

The presence of the grandmothers is something that has always been in our psyches and our subconscious. On some level, we remember the circle of women who have held us throughout time. These are women who held the space for other women to go through the processes, being with women giving birth or at death. That essential holding and supporting role of women has become dislocated and has not been present in our modern lives. Now, we are healing that ourselves, bringing that circle of women back into our awareness and into our lives. The grandmothers are more present in our lives now than they have been for some time.

During more than forty-five years that I have been working, I have always had a circle of grandmothers, there in the unseen realm, watching over us. They help us as women to retrieve our information from which many of us have become dislocated, through materialism and through moving away from tribal traditions. Yet, each one of us carries that information deep within us, in our bones and in our blood.

Traditionally, there were circles of grandmothers holding space and holding rituals. When the Iroquois brokered the 'Great Peace'[*] between five nations of the Native American people, under their constitution the woman elders appointed their chiefs. They had a council of women, always at the ready, to bring important issues and decisions to the attention of the Confederacy Council. Can you imagine if, in today's world, we had circles of women, people like our first Irish female president and UN human rights commissioner, Mary Robinson, who were respected, loved, and were seen as grandmothers, and if they advised our politicians? How different the world would be.

[*]   Iroquois Confederacy Constitution Articles 18,25,37 & 95.
https://www.warpaths2peacepipes.com/native-american-indians/iroquois-confedera-cy-constitution-articles-35-to-54.htm

All over the world, there are women advocating for women to come together to take their role in protecting the future of this planet for those yet to be.

The element of the North is earth, just as the South is fire and the East and the West are air and water. On the Wheel, the North is also the place where the souls reside, waiting to be reborn. In our mythology, Tlachtga collected the souls, they passed over in Samhain and moved on to Tír na nÓg, the land of the forever young, to await rebirth. Their spirits became part of this earth and kept this land green and fertile. The air that we breathe, the colour of the flowers and the butterflies are all part of the spirit of life itself. On the Wheel, the North is the place where the souls reside, waiting for rebirth at Imbolc. This is also the place where they make their contracts with other souls, attract what they need, and choose the environment into which they need to come back. So this is the place of the void. It is the place of the uncreated, a place of energy waiting to take form.

Traditions

The winter solstice (*grianstad an gheimhridh* – literally translated as 'winter sun-stop') is the day of mid-winter. It is the longest night and shortest day of the year. Many see this as the eternal battle between darkness and light. People know that, after this night and day, the ancestors are moving back a step, so we begin to move forward, towards Imbolc. It is a time for our deepest communion within ourselves. Traditionally, people could not travel far around this time and so, they learnt patience as they lived in close quarters with their families. The stories and songs of Samhain began to dwindle from this time on. Communities congregated, to feel the safety of being together and called upon the sun to return and make its way towards them again.

Many people kept their cattle in the cottage or *rath* with them and the warmth of the animals kept the people warm. Evergreens were brought in to decorate the house: holly, ivy and the mystical mistletoe. Some believed that evergreens were a place for nature spirits to rest. People prepared a feast, knowing how much would still be needed for the coming months. Food was shared with others so that those in need were taken care of. At this time, *poitín*, the illegal whiskey, was often ready for its first tasting. A log was decorated in honour of the Cailleach and burned, making way for Brigit. A candle was lit and put by the window so passers-by would know they were welcome at this time. The candle also signified the returning of the light.

On the morning of the winter solstice at Newgrange, one of our oldest sites in Ireland, the rising sun comes through a lintel over the doorway and a growing, lighted pathway penetrates into the inner chamber, until it reaches the triple spiral carved into the rock. This has been happening for at least five thousand years and could well go on for thousands of years to come. One possible interpretation is that of the Sun God, penetrating into the womb, awakening the Ancient Mother to come forth again.

The earth is making her way around again, reminding us of our own journeys in life. People gather to watch the morning sun, knowing that it is a promise of longer days to come. For some, the descent into the dark months is a hard journey and this night and day of the winter solstice brings hope.

The colour of the winter solstice is grey, between the black of Samhain and the white of Imbolc. It is still more black than white.

A Personal Journey with the Cailleach

The Cailleach has always been with me, since I was very young. The first time I came home to Ireland, I was a baby in my mum's arms, only a few months old.

When I visited Granny's as a child, I always ran first and lay in the field. I lay there until I became the field, then the hill and the valley and the mountains. It was then that the old woman came to me. She whispered and talked to me. That mother energy is also the Cailleach.

For me, the Cailleach has always been the land. She is here in my own place, in Kerry. She is in every step I take. Everything on the body of Ireland is a part of her in a different way. As the Cailleach, she is in Clare on the Burren. She is the Hag of Beara in County Cork. There are different personifications of her.

When I turned sixty, I thought it was time for my croning ceremony. I asked two or three women elders if they were free on one date or another and they were not available, so I thought, oh well, I might just do it myself. I went to the grandmother's circle – the stone circle near Killarney. I asked the seven stones, the seven grandmothers, to put me through a croning ceremony. As I went into the journey, I saw them come out and put a black cloak around me. Then, when they stepped back, it was as if they took the outside of the cloak away. I looked down and I was wearing a rainbow cloak. "As you become crone, you are all women. You have been maiden; you have been mother. You are all. You have experienced all. It is not that you are separate from them. You are all."

That is when I realised that all the essences, all the deities come unto the Cailleach. They are all part of her. More and more, my own body and the earth reminds me of the Cailleach. I see crevices and lines on her body, on trees and on stones. I see her folds in the rolling of the land. She has always been here for me in Kerry. This land where I live is my place of sacredness, my sanctuary, my soul home.

Cailleach Béara.
The Hag of Beara, an ancient,
naturally-formed image of the
Cailleach, in West Cork.

WALKING
THE WHEEL

Movement of the Wheel

In my workshops, when we walk the Wheel, I use a circular altar cloth that has the eight points on it. I place the cloth on the floor of the room, with the eight spokes radiating out from the centre, four towards the four corners of the room and the other four towards the mid-points of each of the four walls. We place objects on it to symbolise each of the directions or deities. I orientate the cloth to have Samhain in the Northwest. Our other main points will be Imbolc in the Northeast, Bealtaine in the Southeast and Lughnasa in the Southwest. We familiarise ourselves with these directions, points and deities, and also with the colours of the different segments of the wheel.

We begin walking the circle from Samhain, in a clockwise direction. It is best to walk without shoes, if possible, so that we can feel that electromagnetic grid beneath our feet. The earth is a huge magnet. Each time we lift our feet and step back down on the earth, we plug back into her body. We allow that electromagnetic energy to flow through us. We become conscious of this, allowing that energy to flow through our body as we move, as we lift each foot and place it back on the ground. I usually drum and we walk the circle, no more than three times. As we walk, we feel the direction to which our feet are pulled at this time. There is never a wrong place to stand on the Wheel. The point to which we are drawn is always exactly where we need to be right now. We stand in that place and begin to work with the energy and archetype associated with that point on the wheel.

When we walk the Wheel, we start from Samhain and walk around

103

the eight points of the circle in a sunwise (clockwise) direction, one, two, three, four, five, six, seven, eight, from Northwest, to North to Northeast, to East, and on to Southeast, South, Southwest and West, and round again, always beginning with Samhain in the Northwest. As we walk, we visualise the deities, moving through Tlachtga, the Cailleach, Brigit, Boann, Medb, Áine, Tailtiú, Macha and back again to Tlachtga. We also see the colours, starting with black at Samhain and moving through black, grey, white, pink (or blue if that is the colour we prefer for Boann), red for Bealtaine and on to orange, gold, brown, before returning to black. We walk the circle no more than three times, to sense which section and deity we are drawn towards.

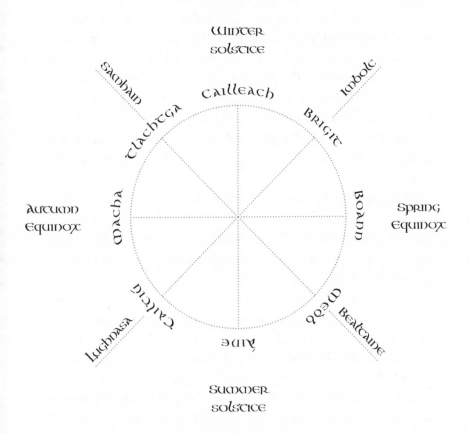

Standing in the Place of Tlachtga

In this place, we are invited to have a closer relationship with Tlachtga and to explore our way of being with her. Once we develop a relationship with Tlachtga, we no longer need to be afraid of death. We are being called to go deep within ourselves, to move into her space and when we allow ourselves to go into that place, she comes to our aid.

Often we are brought up to fear the darkness, yet, it is in that fear of darkness that fear itself grows. Many years ago, near Basel, Germany, I visited a village that was built on the principles of Rudolf Steiner. In the main building they had a room that was pure black. Steiner believed that, when a person got depressed, or even a bit down, they needed to sit in the darkness rather than fight it. They needed to stay in that place to find the light that lies within the darkness.

Once we have developed a relationship with Tlachtga, we do not have to sit in the place of death, because death is always with us. Death shows itself to us in every line of our faces and every fold of our bodies. Awareness of our mortality is not a burden that we carry, rather, it is what makes us value life and live it to the full. In the end, it can often be a relief to go to Tlachtga and know that this place of releasing is always available to us in our lives.

Standing in the place of Tlachtga, we recognise that there are things that we hold and things that hold us. We might not be conscious of them, but we can feel them pulling us. There might be things we carry, right now, that are heavy for us. It could be the death of a relationship, the end of a job, or some process we are going through within ourselves.

Often there are things or people that we have been carrying, that are not ours to carry any longer. If we do not release memories, experiences or emotions that we hold, we attract more of that experience into our lives. What we hold is what we attract electromagnetically.

Whenever we hold on to situations or to people who no longer feed or support us, we lose energy. We call on Tlachtga to assist us in releasing burdens that we carry. We can ask her, "How can I release this, so that I can move on?"

We cannot move on until we have released those burdens. There is no point in waiting for new things to come in before we let go of what we are holding. We have to let go first. It is only by releasing that we attract the new.

Sometimes, we find ourselves in this place because we have not let go of Tlachtga herself. Either we have not finished our work with her, or the work is finished and we have not let go of her. It is important to allow ourselves to move on from this place.

In letting go, we go into the void, which is a powerful place. The void is the place of that which is waiting to be created. It is a place of magic and mystery, where we can draw on all that we need. But, first, we have to allow ourselves to go into the darkness with Tlachtga.

Standing in the Place of the Cailleach

The North is the place of the Cailleach, the place of wisdom. In her own life, and her own time, each woman comes to the point where she must face and embrace the crone within herself. As I discovered at my croning ceremony, we are maiden and mother as well as crone. We do not lose those younger aspects of ourselves: we are all three faces of woman.

Nowadays, many people resist getting old. We no longer sit at the feet of our elders. We have lost a lot of information because of that. Our elders have the stories and, once they are gone, their precious stories are gone too. That is why they often tell the stories again and again, to make sure that we remember because they have been through experiences that we cannot even contemplate.

The grandmothers give us strength; they hold us and guide us at times when we feel bereft or alone. They whisper in our ears. The grandmothers remind us of our nature and our interconnectedness with the land. They knew how to take what was needed and weave it. The grandmothers walked through life, experienced life, grew through life and heard their grandmothers' stories. There is a continuity in us that goes back to the beginning. We carry that within our DNA.

We have a circle of grandmothers who are there to remind us of our stories and our songs and of the ancient wisdom. In this place, they help us to retrieve that information and bring it forth again. As we grow on in life, we can feel them close to us and can choose, if we wish, to allow them to work through us, to share the information that is needed for all of us to hear.

In the North, we can call upon our grandmothers for their wisdom and their wildness. How wonderful to see a really wild, old woman, completely eccentric and in her power. We can claim that wildness for ourselves too, as we grow older.

The North is also the place of the souls waiting to be reborn. When we stand here, we have stepped out of something and have not yet stepped into something new. We are betwixt and between.

Often, we are frightened of being in the void, but the void is actually the place of women. We come from the void and return to the void. The void is full of potential. We think somewhere is empty because we do not see what is there. Space is filled with energy and the void is too. It is filled with all of that potential waiting for us to draw from it.

When we allow ourselves to sit in the void, we really embrace our power as women. We embrace all the creative magic and energy that we hold within us. Our purpose on this planet is to create, not just children of the body but children of the mind.

To enter the void, we let go and step inside, closing the door behind us. We cannot carry anything in with us, because we may carry that into the next experience. Things need to be a bit foggy at first. By allowing ourselves to be in the fog and giving gratitude for the lack of clarity, we can find that the fog brings us more than we had anticipated or expected. We can put power and energy into it, so that, when it clears, it will be magic.

How powerful it is to allow ourselves to sit in that place and space of unknowing. It is the place where energy waits to take form. We need to just be in it, knowing that something will manifest and that, when it is ready, the impulse within us will begin to move us forward.

In today's world, how many of us can spend time in the void, when we are so pressurised into doing? I recently saw an advertisement for pills to let you get more done in one day. And I thought, oh my gosh, more? The reason we are being pressurised not to sit in the void is because we become so powerful when we are in that place.

Usually, when we finish something, we want to jump into something new, whether it's a job, a relationship, or an understanding that we have suddenly gained. We have all met somebody who has just gained an insight and wants to grab it and do something with it right now. Each one of us needs to sit in the place of the North, to reside in the void for a little while, so that we can take on all that we have been and have worked through, before we are ready to step forward. Invariably, we will move forward because the wheel turns. I remember spirit saying once, "You're no longer on a path, you're on an escalator". And we are. The world is moving at such a fast pace, we all need to take that respite.

We need to take that space of letting things rest before we move into something new. When we finish a relationship, we need to take that rest, that grace of being, before we move on. Otherwise we cannot take in all that we have learnt. The waves come in and the waves go out. We need that ebb and flow too. The North teaches us to rest awhile.

The door has to close behind us before the door in front of us will open. Sometimes that can feel a bit frightening, being in the place of unknowing. Having that space, we do not have to have the answer to everything. The answers lie within; we just have to allow them to evolve through us as we sit in that place of being. We are not limiting ourselves by being there. If we move straight away from one thing to another, we keep ourselves within a certain energetic field. We do not allow that field to expand or that energy to release. Being in that void is having the grace to let things shift and move. Only then will we be ready. That life force, that light within us, will move us to where we need to be.

Standing here, this is a space for waiting and transition. We have been through a death or release and are moving towards rebirth; we are drawn towards that new place, but are not there yet. In this place of transition, changes are occurring in our lives. We need to recognise those changes, honour them and allow ourselves to flow with them.

The winter solstice is also the place of connecting to the earth. How does each one of us connect personally with the earth? Are we aware of walking on the earth and of her changing seasons? How aware are we of this earth that lives and breathes to give us life? We are reminded that to live and breathe should be to participate in her life. In this place we are being told that we need to connect with the earth. We are also reminded that we are held by spirit. Spirit is there and will hold us in the place of the Cailleach.

From the void, we move into the place of birth with Brigit.

Standing in the Place of Brigit

Brigit holds this space, the place of birth and beginnings. This is the time when the seed is put into the ground and begins to grow. It is the place of seeding things. Standing in this place, it tells us that we have been through a time of darkness and through the void. Empowered by that experience, we have come to the place of beginning again.

It asks us what seeds we want to sow. What do we want to grow in our future? This is a time to look at all that lies within the seed and all that can grow from it. From the acorn, great oaks can grow. From the seed of our ideas, amazing things can flourish. We can call upon Brigit to help us with that.

This is the place of beginning, of birth, of new things coming into our lives. We need to be open to that. Brigit midwifes things into being. She is the one we call on when we want to give birth, both physical birth and creations of the mind. She is the patroness of the arts.

When we stand in the place of Brigit, we ask for new things to come into our lives: new opportunities, new awareness. We are called to allow ourselves to move and change and to wear many hats. How do we wear those hats? How do we dance our dance?

As the wheel turns, we move from the place of birth with Brigit into the place of Boann, the place of the young girl, innocence and vitality.

Standing in the Place of Boann

The place of Boann, in the East, is between birth and flowering. It used to be the place of the young girl growing up and preparing for flowering. Nowadays it is first blood, because girls are bleeding so much younger. Some girls of eight and nine are bleeding and are often not ready for it. They are not mature enough, sexually awake or aware. For them, this part of childhood is getting caught up in their youth.

The East is the place of innocence, the place of first dreams. Young girls begin to cultivate their creativity. Creativity could be hunting, engineering, cooking, painting, writing, working with animals or people, dancing, singing, or making jewellery – whatever way they find to express themselves. We cannot limit creativity. This place of innocence is a time of finding what moves them, what they enjoy and what begins to awaken them, so that, when they go into Bealtaine, they are already prepared and can come into their own and find their passion. They can find that flowering in Bealtaine. Then, when they meet a partner, they come together in a place of wholeness, not in a place of loss. They know who they are and know the dreams they carry.

If we need to retrieve aspects of ourselves as the child or the young girl, we go to the place of Boann. If abuse of any type happens to young girls, we sit with them and hold them in this space and place. Traditionally, it was a time when young girls began to move from playing with the children and started to help the women of the tribe.

Between the ages of seven and fifteen, we dream of our future selves. I used to dream of being a famous film star. A huge black car would stop one day, the door would open and someone would say, "You are just who we are looking for". We have all had those dreams.

The place of Boann is our dreaming time. Dream is almost essential to our nature. Yet, in the types of education to which most of us were exposed, we could have been smacked or punished for dreaming, or told not to dream. Some women find themselves out of balance because they have never allowed themselves to dream.

This is the place of remembering the dreams that we carry, opening to our dreams, working with them and bringing them to fruition. If we do not dream, we can go the opposite way and get depressed. We need to know that we can dream and dream true, using our dream time to bring what we need into our own reality. If we have decisions to make, we can put them into the dream time. We can see ourselves following that path. Where will it lead? How will it open for us? Then we come back to this time and space. And then we dream into that other path. Where will that path take us? How will that open for us? And then we come back and try to feel, which one do I want to look back on when I am in my nineties and say, "I'm glad I did that"? Boann will help us to dream things true for ourselves.

Boann helps us to access the inner child and learn to play again. Some of us did not play enough when we were young. Were we able to be the child? Was the inner child able to play? Do we know how to play? Can we just let go and not take life so seriously? Boann calls us to play. If we do not play, we can fall back into ourselves, fall ill or fall down. The melancholy starts because we are not able to access that playfulness of youth within us. She can help us to find that child again.

Boann's element is water. Each of us grows in our mother's waters and are fed through the placenta. After birth, we go again to the waters of our Great Mother, to be blessed. What does water mean for us? Water is emotion, feeling, cleansing and dreaming.

As women we need to be aware that our feelings are our tools. We need to acknowledge what we feel and what our feelings are telling us when we go into a place and meet people. What sensations are we picking up? Boann helps us to recognise that and work with it.

Boann, the great river goddess, brings that river energy through us, allowing us to move. Water can break through anything. We need to know that everything flows and we can let go of anything that we are holding. We can just let it flow. All things will come to us, because the river feeds us and will continue to flow. That is what Boann tells us as we stand in this place.

From the place of innocence, we move into the place of passion with Medb.

Standing in the Place of Medb

As Imbolc was the seed, Bealtaine is the flower, the time of flowering and awakening to our passion.

Medb is powerful, passionate and wild. In today's world, the name Medb means wanton and hussy, because it is said that Medb could have thirty-two men in a night and still be found wanting.

It is the place where our passion awakens. What are we passionate about? What makes us know that we are alive? What makes us wake up in the morning and want to be alive? What is our passion? What moves us? What motivates us in life? What gets us going? The place of Medb is about finding that passion, opening to it and living in that passion – eating and drinking of life. Do we actually participate in life, or do we only watch life as it goes by? Medb is calling us to eat and drink of life. When we live life like that, it is powerful.

Bealtaine is the flowering of the young woman, when she awakens to her sexual energies, the time when she begins to find that space, that place within herself. It is the time of first lovemaking and when she awakens to ecstasy and bliss. Through that, she awakens to her own magic, finding that passion within herself. It is also the flowering of ourselves. We do not hold back or hide our talents, but allow them to flourish and grow.

Standing in the place of Medb, it is a time to explore and awaken our passion. In the Catholic and other patriarchal traditions, a woman did not have sexual passion let alone any other type. Bealtaine is about finding our passion and embracing it. When we awaken to our passion, whether that is sexual passion or passion for anything else that we love to do, we awaken to the vibration of life. We begin to hear our own heartbeat and to feel our pulse. When we feel our own pulse, feel that life flowing through us, we connect with the earth as well. We have a right to pleasure. When we allow our passion to flow, we are truly alive.

This is the place of the chalice, the Holy Grail. And of course, the chalice is the symbol of our womb. Our bleeding time is the time of our magic, the magic that lies within us as women. Bealtaine is a celebration of our ability to create life.

We go to Medb to awaken our passion and find our power. When we believe in something and need to hold to it no matter what, we call on Medb. She helps us to keep that clarity and focus. It is easy to get worn down sometimes and Medb allows us the opportunity to break through that. She can wake us up. If we are looking for a partner, we might call on Medb.

Bealtaine is also the place of the sacred marriage, the union of one to another (as in the chieftain and the land) and also the union within ourselves. It is where we can balance our feminine and our masculine. We can open both sides of our nature and, by honouring each, we can come to the place of sacred marriage within ourselves.

From Bealtaine, we move into the place of Áine, the place of the impregnation of the fire of the sun into the fruit: a place of ripening.

Standing in the Place of Áine

The place of Áine is the fire within us. Just as we found our passion with Medb at Bealtaine, we find our fire with Áine at the summer solstice. Fire can burn us or keep us warm. It can also bring inspiration. At times, we feel low and limp and need to cultivate our fire. Fire is bright. Sometimes we are frightened by that in ourselves, or in other people. Fire can be too much for us and so we draw back from the brightness. Áine helps us to find the fire within ourselves and to celebrate it in others. Even if we cannot be in it with them, we can celebrate their expression of their fire. Sometimes, in the place of Áine, we take on too much fire and burn out quickly. She helps us to balance that.

When we try to create but something is missing, we go to Áine for inspiration. We can stand in our own inspiration and hold to that light, knowing that we are in the place of the sun.

As the fruit grows, Áine brings the life force into it. When we stand in the place of Áine, we awaken to that life force and recognise that magic is all around us. We open ourselves to that magical energy, recognising that we are part of that magic and need it in our lives. The world also needs magic.

When we fall in love and have that energy and excitement, we feel high, alive and awake. That is the energy of Áine. She brings the element of fun, excitement and movement, that sense of being fully awake.

Being in the place of Áine, it is a time of activity and energy. We can build our energy, work with it and allow ourselves to move into that place of betwixt and between. It is telling us not to be too intense and caught up in logic. There is more to life than we can see.

Áine is the fairy queen. They say that on Midsummer's Day the veil between our world and the fairy realm is at its thinnest. In Ireland the fairy folk are very present among us. The old people still talk about them and there are places like fairy forts which we cannot disturb. This is the place of connecting to the elementals. We can call on the fairies and nature spirits, get to know them and work with them. If we leave part of our garden overgrown, maybe with wildflowers, leave gifts for the fairies and call upon them, they might come and work with us to beautify that place. We can have them in our garden and play with them.

In the stories, Áine has three faces – the fairy queen, the mermaid and the old woman. In this place, we can also be like a child and like an elder, though it is very much a place of playing with magic.

Sometimes Áine pulls us out of this world a little and into the fairy realm. She does not always hold us here and we have to be aware of that. But if we feel too grounded or stuck and cannot move out, if we need some imagination or magic in our lives, then we go to Áine to help with that.

From the summer solstice, we move into the place of the harvest and the fruit with Tailtiú at Lughnasa.

Standing in the Place of Tailtiú

Things that we began at the time of Imbolc, that reached their flowering at the time of Bealtaine, are ready for harvesting now. At the time of harvest, we gather the fruits of our labour, our gifts. It is a time of recognising the work we have put into things. What we have put out is coming back to us. We do not let that pass us by, we use it. This is a time for us to gather and use all the gifts that we have. We walk forward, and use those gifts in a way that fulfils us and stimulates our creativity.

In the place of Lughnasa, we draw on the gifts with which we were born and start to use and cultivate them. We receive, now, from all we have learnt in life. Every single thing that we have experienced in life is part of our teachings and part of who we are. This is the time to start receiving from all we have worked through in life. Standing in this place, we look and think: what can we do now with all the gifts that we have got and all the things that we have learnt? Where can we go with all of this now? We ask Tailtiú for help with that.

The place of Tailtiú is also a place of inner and outer healing for ourselves. It is here that we bring healing to others, through words or actions, or just by being or bearing witness. As we hold that space for others, Tailtiú holds that space for us.

Lughnasa is the place of the gentle, grace-filled mother. Whereas Medb brings us passion and power, Tailtiú brings us grace. As women we had to go on quite a journey in the last hundred years to reclaim our passion and power. We do not want to lose our grace either. Grace can be easily abused in a woman. That gentle, nurturing nature is something that we need to recognise in ourselves and in our roots. We need to honour our grace, make space for it and respect it.

Tailtiú died from her labours and, when we take a mothering role, we need to remember not to give all of ourselves. We must always feed and care for ourselves and water what we have grown. How do we mother ourselves? Do we take the space to do what needs to be done for us? If we mother others, who mothers us? From where do we receive our nourishment? Are we open to receiving? I remember spirit saying to me many years ago, "Blessed are those who give and thrice blessed are those who receive".

Many women are trained into motherhood from the time the doctor tells their mothers that they are female. We are trained to be nurturers, carers and holders. Sometimes we miss out on other parts of ourselves because of that. When we come to the place of Lughnasa, the gentle mother, we recognise the mother within us. Mothering is a face that is a part of us all, whether we have children or not. But it is only a part, not the whole. We also have a wild woman, a Medb and the brightness, the Brigit.

Some of us give mothering at the time when we most need it ourselves. Unconsciously we put that out hoping to receive it back. Because of that, we can build up resentment as well as giving false love. This place tells us that we must learn to recognise and acknowledge our own needs. We accept that it is our right, as human beings and as women, to have those needs fulfilled.

The place of Tailtiú is where we go to be mothered, held and loved. It is important that we do not fall into the role of the mother, in the sense of constantly holding people. Sometimes, when we hold a person for too long, they become dependent on us. That causes difficulty for us and the relationship. It is always important, in the place of Lughnasa, not to be over-nurturing but to recognise that, like every animal, we have to watch the young grow. Birds kick the young out of the nest to get them flying. People can become dependent on us and not want to move on because they get used to that dependency. On another level, standing in that space, we also need to be held. It tells us to make sure that we have friends around us, a group of sisters, or people who can nourish and hold us when we need it. We can ask Tailtiú for support in that.

From the place of the harvest with Tailtiú, we move on to the place of the indwelling cave, the place of Macha.

Standing in the Place of Macha

The two stories of Macha represent different parts of ourselves. In one, she died because silence was not kept. In the other, she fought. There are times when we keep silent and close down for fear of retribution or loss. We can have silence imposed on us by religion or society. There can be silence imposed on us as women. It may have been passed on to us through our mothers, from them, or from the generations of women before them who were silenced. At other times, we can draw upon what is within us, to fight or to claim what is ours – to speak our truth.

In this place of Macha, we can be pushed into a situation where we can allow ourselves to die a little, or we can choose to fight, sometimes alone. Macha can help us to know when to bend and when to hold our ground.

Standing in the place of Macha, it is a time of introspection and reflection. Macha draws us in to find what lies within us. The autumn equinox, the place of Macha, is the point on the wheel where we have the indwelling cave, the place of our becoming or undoing.

From early childhood, each one of us creates a cave within us. Our cave holds those aspects of ourselves that we do not like, or of which we are ashamed. It can hold experiences that were too difficult for us to cope with, maybe because of our age, or because of the circumstances at that time of our lives. We are taught, verbally and non-verbally, that some parts of our nature are not acceptable to our family or to society, so we hide those aspects of ourselves.

When we do not go into that cave, it becomes the place of our undoing because those hidden parts are not integrated into ourselves. If we can bring those parts into our nature, then it can be the place of our becoming, empowering us to become all that we can be.

Growing up, we might have been told that it was wrong to be angry or wild, so we hide it away, deep within ourselves. There was a woman I knew for whom it was her laughter. As a child, she threw her head back and laughed and her parents told her that she would be put into an institution. She learnt to close down that laughter until she reached the stage where she was afraid to open her mouth. She became very ill with ME – chronic fatigue syndrome – and had not done the work that, as a young woman, she had been inspired to do.

Sometimes we forget what we have put into that cave. It contains parts of ourselves that we do not want to see and experiences that we do not want to remember. We are so protective of that cave that each one of us attracts an animal guide or helper to guard it for us. It could be a bear, a lion, a snake or a dragon. Woe betide anyone who tries to get in there. Our animal will go for them. At times, we can see that animal in others. If we confront them with something, we can see their animal in the words that come out of their mouths.

Over time, we can forget that we created that cave for ourselves and that our own animal helper protects it. We can become frightened of that place and of the unresolved emotions that we could unleash by going there. When we need to access that cave for ourselves, we often have to fight the animal that guards it.

Every one of us has an animal protecting that part and those aspects of ourselves that we have hidden. Often, we forget that it is our own animal, our own reflection. We have to embrace that part of ourselves and not attempt to kill it. Our animal nature is strong and determined to survive and we need it for our survival.

We need our instinct to tell us when something is wrong. Our animal nature does not have intelligence; it just knows something does not feel right. That does not necessarily mean it is dangerous for us. Our instinct does not know the difference. We have to stop and ask ourselves, what am I feeling? The second question we ask is: has it anything to do with me? I am feeling strange energy in this place – does it have to do with me? If the answer is no, that is okay. As soon as we begin to ask that question, we open a dialogue between the instinct and the intellect and that allows the instinct to feed us the necessary information. Rather than fighting our animal nature, we need to embrace and love it, but we cannot allow it to rule us. We would never let our dog rule us; we know we need to discipline it. The same is true of our own animal, our inner being.

When we have embraced our animal self, we can go into that place of darkness to look at what we are hiding from ourselves and the world. We can bring light into the cave to see what we hold and what parts of our nature were denied expression. We can bring love, understanding and compassion and embrace all that we hold and all those things that we do not like about ourselves. Anger is not bad in itself. It is only destructive if we let it have its nature. Our anger can tell us that something is inappropriate or unacceptable. If we are angry, we need to recognise that we feel angry. That does not mean that we act on that anger, it means that we recognise and honour it. When we do that, we integrate aspects of ourselves rather than cutting them off. It strengthens us to know that part of our nature.

Nothing within us is negative, evil or wrong. It is part of us and is there for a reason. When we embrace all that we are in our ferociousness, anger, melancholy and wildness, this is the place of our becoming.

The place of Macha is opposite the place of Boann on the Wheel. Whereas the East is innocence and cultivating creativity, the West is where we can go crazy if we cannot express our creativity. If women are not allowed to live out the truth of who they are, they can close down and close in. In this place of undoing, they can go crazy.

If we do not go into that cave, it becomes the cave of our undoing, because there are parts of ourselves that are not integrated into the rest and, without them, we can never become whole. We go into the cave to really look at what we have been hiding from ourselves and from the world. On the surface, we can be all sweetness and light and, all the time, underneath, we can be moaning and bitching to ourselves about things.

If we do not go into that cave and acknowledge or incorporate those aspects of ourselves, they will always take from us. Life will never feed us because we are using so much creative energy to guard that cave, rather than drawing and attracting what we need in life. If we do not allow ourselves to go into that cave, we will never be in balance. People will always be a threat, because we are not sure what they will evoke in us. If we do not go into our cave, it can be the place of our undoing.

Standing in the place of the cave we are called to look at what we hold. We are asked to look at the programmes that were given to us when we were growing up and to revisit those aspects of ourselves that felt shameful or fearful to us. Can we go in there and recognise all that is? If we bring that into the light, there is nothing there to pull from us, to make us fearful or to take energy from us. Nothing is negative. It is just energy. By going into that cave and seeing what is there, we allow that energy to move and flow, empowering us to become all that we can be.

Macha is there to help us to go into our cave, to open to our power, to fight for our selves and to fight for what is right. Macha teaches us that we can do that by standing in our power. She is there to hold and teach us. Macha is the cousin of Medb. They are strong archetypes and strong women.

On the Wheel, the autumn equinox is opposite the place of the young girl in the East. It is the place of a woman's change of life (normally in her forties), when her periods are slowing down. She is no longer giving birth for the good of the tribe. It is the time of gathering her own gifts, the time of finding what she wants to work with for herself.

Being opposite the place of innocence, this can also be the crazy place, the place of the crazy woman. If we find ourselves stuck and beginning to go crazy, we need to go into the cave and be crazy. We can go into the cave and sit in the darkness and let the craziness out for a while, rather than resisting or fighting it. That way, we can let ourselves balance. Part of the gift of getting older is that we do not need permission to be crazy.

When we embrace all that we are and stand in the presence of our truths, we become all that we can be. We stand in our power. That prepares us to move forward into Samhain and into Tlachtga. When we finally reach that gate, we do not want to carry regret. We want to know that we have lived life.

From the place of Macha, we move back to Samhain, back to the place of darkness and decay. The wheel turns full circle.

Working with the Wheel

The Wheel is a tool that we can use as we journey in life. We can walk the wheel and see where we are at any point in our lives, on our journey with a person, with a relationship, with an experience, or whatever we need to clarify. At any time, we can ask a deity to step forward to guide us. That archetype will help us to see that situation more clearly. Through working with the Wheel, we can embrace all those archetypal aspects of ourselves. We can embrace the darkness with the Cailleach, the playful child with Boann, the gentle mother with Tailtiú, reclaim our passion with Medb, develop our third eye with Brigit, encounter the fairy realms with Áine or release our burdens to Tlachtga. With Macha, we can go into the cave and recognise what we are holding or what we are being pressurised to hide. It is a powerful process. As we move round and round the Wheel, things evolve and we ourselves evolve.

When we continuously walk and work with the Wheel, the deities and archetypes become part of us. As we become one with ourselves, we move to the centre of our own circle and become conscious of the deities all around us. All we need to do is to turn one way or the other to call upon them, because they are there. We have already forged that relationship with them. They have become like good friends that we bring with us into each new situation in our lives.

At the end of each session working with the Wheel, the imagery that is often given to me is of a wraparound skirt. We can think of the Wheel laid out on the floor like a skirt with coloured segments: black, grey, white, pink, red, amber, gold and brown. Then we can imagine that skirt wrapping around us, tight at the waist and the wider end of the circle swirling out around us. As we turn and turn at the end, we can gradually feel all those energies and colours wrap themselves around us. That is how it always finishes for me, somehow. I am wrapped and held within it, almost as if the Wheel were three-dimensional.

The Spiral Path

We have seen the Wheel and worked with it in a two-dimensional way. In the shamanic tradition, the Wheel is also seen three-dimensionally, as a spiral. We are born at a specific point on the Wheel and that is where we begin. The deity at that point holds that space for us. As the Wheel turns and we go round and round, we walk a spiral path in life. We walk the spiral several times, returning again and again to the point where we began. Whatever we go through, whatever experiences we have in life, we will revisit them again on some level. Every now and then we go through pivotal times of change and transformation. When we do, it is as if we shift up to a different level on that spiral. It is a powerful process.

We go through certain experiences, certain processes, certain teachings in life. If we take responsibility, if we are able to respond rather than react to each situation, then we grow through our experiences and they become our teachings. As we take responsibility within each situation we move through that. Then, our path does not just go around the Wheel two-dimensionally, it spirals up three-dimensionally, so we can leapfrog up to the next level.

If we do not take responsibility, or we do not take on that teaching, we can be held in that place. Then, that aspect of us can be like a record that gets stuck, that experience stays with us. We continue to attract that into our lives until we deal with it, if we ever do.

When we have dealt with that situation or experience, we will be tested, because that is part of our psyche in this planet. We have to go through a driving test to drive. We have to do certain exams to be qualified to do specific jobs. The universe will test us. I do not mean some universe outside of ourselves, some outer entity. We will be tested by our soul nature. Something will come back to test us. Depending on whether we respond or react to that, we can release it. Then we can move forward and upward. If we react, we go back into that situation and continue with that teaching.

After we have cleared the energies of that experience, we might revisit it on another level and bear witness, either through someone else or by helping somebody on their path. That is all part of the spiral.

In the apprentice work, when the participants have completed the different levels and are ready, they 'Walk the Spiral'. This is a powerful teaching which takes approximately five days and allows them to make/take that shift on to the next level of their journey. When the apprentices get to that level and walk the spiral, everything in their life shifts and it is wonderful to behold.

IMMRAMA

I) IREL(AD) I) OUR CI)ÌÒÒlE CLORlò.
this reality, we have what is called the immram (in Irish *iomramh*).
Immrama are journeys, on which we embark and, from which we can
never return. We have several well-known stories of immrama. The
following is the Story of Bran.

The Story of Bran

Bran was the youngest of seven boys. He lived with his brothers,
mother and father in a small fishing village in the West of Ireland. It
was a good life, but it was hard. In the West of Ireland, in Connema-
ra, it is very rocky and it is hard to cultivate the land there. They had
to get up before dawn every morning and go out to fish and they did
not come back until late afternoon.

Bran was forever daydreaming. He was never quick enough. His
father worried about him. He worried that Bran would never be able
to marry and keep a family if he could not do this job. His brothers
were all much bigger than him and stronger, so they pushed and
shoved him around and they took his food. Bran never really cared.
He lived in the world of daydreams. His mother worried a lot about
him and tried to protect him, but she knew the father was right and
that Bran had to learn to be in the here and now. He had to learn to
fish and take care of himself. How would he do that in years to come?

Sometimes, in the evenings, he went out of the little cottage and up
on to the hills. He lay on his belly and looked over the cliff, down at
the sea and watched it crashing on the rocks below. He dreamed of
going to other places. He dreamed of being a seagull and flying off.

He dreamed of being a fish and being able to traverse the seas.

One evening, as he lay there dreaming, he heard music. At first he thought it was the song of a bird, so sweet it was. He thought he was dreaming it. When he opened his eyes he could still hear the music, he could still hear the singing. He pulled himself over to the edge and looked down. Sitting there, on the rocks below him, was the most beautiful woman he had seen in his whole life. Her hair was long and thick and wavy, the colour of honey. Her face was looking up at the evening sky and he could see these rich, red, ruby lips and these eyes that were as blue as the sea itself. His heart quickened and beat as he looked down at her. He closed his eyes to listen to the singing. The next thing he knew, it was early morning. He was stiff and damp. Oh Jesus, what was his father going to say now?

Running back down, he could see his brothers already outside preparing. He ran to them. "Where have you been Bran?" they asked, irritated that he had not been there to do his job again. He did not ' say anything; he knew it was best not to tell them. He kept thinking of that beautiful dream he had.

That evening, when everything became quiet, he slipped out and went again to the top of the hill and lay there. He thought, if I could remember that dream, if I could remember the way she sang… Then, suddenly, he could hear it again. He looked down and he saw her again, sitting on the rocks, her thick wavy hair all around her body and she looking up at the sky, singing away. He was transfixed, mesmerised by her. He closed his eyes. And next thing he knew, again it was early morning. Again his body felt cramped and damp. He got up and went running down. The boys had not even noticed he was not there.

That night he could not stop himself from going out. He could not stop himself from going up. His heart was beating in his chest as he lay down. As he lay there, he heard the singing. His eyes were open, he was pinching himself. He looked over the edge and, as he looked over, he saw these two, big, blue eyes looking up at him. He pulled himself back. He was starting to sweat. He could feel his heart almost coming out of his chest. And he heard laughter. "Bran," she said, "did you not think I knew you were up there watching me?" "Who are you?" he said. "Where do you come from?"

"Come and visit us in Tír na nÓg."

Tír na nÓg is the land of the forever young which lies far off to the West, where the Tuath Dé live. It is the place of forever summer.

"How would I get there?" he said.

"Here," she said and took, from behind her, a silver branch with a thick, heavy, big, red apple hanging off the branch. Before he could do anything, she threw it up and, instinctively, he put his hand out and caught it.

"How can this be?" he said, "for it's just spring time. Where did this apple come from?" The apples were not going to be there 'til the autumn. And the silver branch had green leaves upon it. "Where did this come from?"

"Ah sure, you know where it comes from, Bran," she said. "When you're ready," she said, "build your *currach* and hold that branch out before you in the *currach* and it will guide you to me. And whenever you are hungry or thirsty, take a bite out of the apple and it will quench your thirst, it will take away your hunger."

He did not know what to do.

"Oh but, my family, my parents…" He looked back down to talk to her and she was gone. And here he was sitting with this silver branch and this rich, red apple hanging from it. He was frightened. He was perplexed. He did not know what to do.

He took the branch down and, outside the village, he found a pile of stones. He took some out and put the branch in there with the apple. He put stones back in front of it and thought, I'll leave that for a week or two and it will go rotten. The creatures will come and eat it.

Those days were the hardest days of his life. He worked so hard, and could barely eat with tiredness at night, so that he would not have to think about that silver branch out there behind the stones. He would not have to think about the apple, he would not have to think about that beautiful young woman with those rich, ruby lips and those beautiful blue eyes.

His father was delighted and his brothers stopped bullying him.

After ten days or so, he went out in the evening. His heart was thumping as he took the stones away. He put his hand in, expecting to find something shrivelled. But there was no smell. And out he pulled the silver branch with the green leaves upon it and the rich, red apple.

Bran went to see his best friend, Séamus, took him to the stones and showed him the silver branch with the beautiful, red apple.

"You must cross your heart and promise me that you will not tell another living soul," he said.

Séamus looked at it and his eyes grew wide. And Bran told him his story. At first, Séamus found it very hard to believe, but there in front of him was the living proof: the branch, the leaves and the apple.

Then, Bran began noticing some of the other young lads in the village looking at him, talking quietly and going silent when he got close. He caught hold of Séamus.

"Séamus, did you tell anybody about that branch and that apple?"

"You couldn't carry a story like that on your own," said Séamus, "some of the lads want to go with you. This is a great adventure, man. We could all go."

Bran and the boys from the village decided they would build a *currach* – a very small boat with the central part of wood, like a backbone with ribs up around it. The skin is put over it and is painted with tar. The boys worked on it every night when their parents and their siblings thought they were sleeping. Luckily, the older men were using tar to fix up some of their *currachs*, so it didn't seem unusual that they would have a smell of tar upon them. Eventually, it was ready. It was hidden and it was ready.

Spring had come and gone. They were moving into summer.

"Let's go now, Bran," they said, "so we can be back before the autumn. Let's go, let's go!"

Five of them went at the dead of night. Just as the tide was turning, they pushed the boat out, so the water would draw them out. Bran went and stood at the front of the *currach* and held up the silver branch. And sure enough it moved his arm over. So they rowed that way and they rowed for many days. Every time they got hungry, or they got thirsty, they took a bite of the apple.

One of the days, they met Manannán Mac Lir, the god of the sea.

He saw this tiny craft and asked them, "What are you doing here in my sea?"

"We're going to Tír na nÓg," said Bran.

"Oh," said Manannán, "I see. I see your silver branch, go on with you."

And on they went.

Eventually, they saw the outline of an island. The sun was bursting down upon it. They could see in the distance one person standing there on the beach. They began to row harder and Bran, holding the silver branch, was pulling them closer. He saw her and she saw him. He waved and she waved back. But they could not seem to get in. They could not seem to get into that inlet at all. So, she took out a ball of wool, opened it and tied the end of it to her finger. She threw it out to him and he caught it. And he held it tight, as she pulled them in on to the beach. They pulled up the boat and kept it safe. She took them on to the island. They had never seen land like this, so rich, so green. Everything was in blossom. All the fruits were hanging heavy from the trees. All the people were happy, shining, shimmering, laughing and singing. There was food and drink for all. And, of course, Bran kissed his lady love and that night he lay with her.

They sang and danced and ate for three days and three nights. At the end of that, one of the boys came to Bran.

"Bran, we should go back. I'm worried about my mother. She's a widow now and my brothers are good, but she might need my help. This has been a great adventure, but we need to get back."

"Oh," said Bran, "stay longer, stay longer."

But the lad's concern had got the other boys worried and they too wanted to go back. Bran went to his lady love and said he must go.

"Ah sure, Bran," she said, "you can't go back. Ye have eaten our food and drunk our wine, you can't go back."

"We must," he insisted. "They're worried about their brothers and sisters and their parents. They must go back."

No matter what she said, he was clear. It was his responsibility. He had brought them there and he had to bring them back.

The silver branch was still lying in the boat.

"I'll be back, my love," he promised her. He had no intention of going back to that village himself, but he wanted to take the boys home. So they went back out on the sea. They were much quicker getting back than they had been finding the island. It was not many days before they were coming back again into their own little piece of beach. They recognised everything there.

As they were coming in, they saw people on the beach.

"Who are those people?" they said to each other, "I don't recognise them."

The people on the beach were looking out at these boys, wondering what they were doing. The boys were getting more and more excited and aggravated by these strange people who were on their beach collecting their mussels and their cockles. One of the boys jumped out of the boat and began to swim to the shore. As soon as he got on to the beach, his body fell down and, within minutes, crumbled into dust. The people on the beach stepped back. "What magic is this?" they said.

The boys were silent in the *currach*. Then Bran stood up.

"Who are you?" he asked.

"We live here!" they replied.

"How can you live here?" he said, "I don't recognise you."

"Who are you?" they said.

"I am Bran. Son of Cul."

"Son of Cul? Bran?" A tall, tall young man, came forward. "I am a Cul," he said. "We have no Bran in our family."

"Sure, I don't recognise you," said Bran.

The young man was standing there and he was thinking. "You know," he said. "There was a Bran. We did have a Bran in our family but that was about three hundred years ago." So Bran told them the story. And then they turned their *currach*, held out their silver branch and were never seen or heard of again.

That story is an immram – a journey and a quest. Bran went on an immram and, when one goes on such a journey, one can never come back the same. Oisín went to Tír-na-nÓg with Niamh of the golden hair and she told him that he could only return on condition that he did not dismount from his horse. When his feet, accidentally, touched the land of Ireland, he became an old, old man, because he could never return as the man that he had been.

The important element of immrama is that, like Bran or Oisín, we are changed. That is what happens when we awaken consciously. We cannot go back to sleep, we cannot pretend any more. Once someone realises that their husband is an alcoholic, they cannot go back to not knowing. Some part of them will always know that.

After an immram, we can never go back, we can only go forward. We often have to lose things to go on. Sometimes we lose friends or a relationship and sometimes we cultivate a relationship. It brings great change. There is always a loss and a gain with the immram. It does not always mean that we let go of a relationship, but we can lose our attachment to it. We often love better, more freely and fully, because of that. Attachments can keep us tied into emotional insecurity.

Every experience takes us forward on our journey. Sometimes, when we go through experiences that awaken us, it can be difficult to go back into situations where people expect us to be the same as we were. We might try to go back but we cannot, because we have changed. The immram allows us to recognise that, as souls, we are capable of staying awake and making conscious choices. We recognise the importance of those choices because they affect the generations that come after us.

The immram is a very strong journey tool. When we prepare for an immram, we build our *currach* from our bones. Our vertebrae become the backbone of the *currach* and our ribs become its ribs. The *currach* carries and protects us, just as our own ribs and backbones protect our hearts.

Traditionally, swan (and sometimes heron) feathers were worn to journey. The shaman might make a cloak of feathers and put that over the person who was journeying. A loosely woven blanket or crochet shawl could have feathers stuck into it and could be used instead.

A Modern Immram

In my workshops and apprentice groups, we embark on an immram where we build our *currach* and travel together across the sea to Tír na nÓg. People are waiting there to gift us stories, words and memories. We are welcomed and receive their gifts before they, gently, bring us back to the shore and push our boat out into the sea. As we go forth on our journey, we carry with us all that we have received in words, feelings, thoughts and senses. This journey brings us to the land where we live and the people we know. We go forth, rather than back, because one can never return from such a journey.

As we approach our homeland, we meet some of the people we love and have loved. We acknowledge the gifts that they gave us, the gift of life or the gift of teachings we gained through them. We thank them and release any ties that keep us bound to them, realising that we never release the ties of love.

By letting go, we gift ourselves permission to move forward in all that we are, shedding things that no longer belong to us. We are not held or restricted and will not attract those situations into our lives again. Instead, we choose to walk forward unencumbered, connected to others through love and by choice.

Here, too, we acknowledge that we are exactly where we need to be and do not need to carry others. We give ourselves permission to trust our own soul, so that we can live in harmony with ourselves, being true to our soul's purpose.

As we come ashore, we thank our shipmates and move gently back into our own bodies.

I have recorded Bran's story and an immram in my own voice. To journey with it, please visit: https://www.celticsouljourneys.com/seabhean-journeys/#immram

MIDDLE
WORLD TOOLS

As well as the Wheel and the immram, there are many other tools available to us in the Middle World, to assist us to be all that we are meant to be. The following is a list of shamanic tools in my tradition that was shared with me by the ancient ones and which we use here in Ireland. These are part of my teachings. I have not delved into other shamanic traditions and I believe that my teachings are authentic to Ireland, because this is where I learned them, journeying with the Stone People, the tree brethren and the Tuath Dé, who have shown them to me.

Living Earth Tools

Stewardship of the Land

The Irish have always had a close relationship with the land, from the time when we moved from being hunters and began to care for and cultivate the soil. We have always respected the land and understood that, if we take care of the land, it will support and feed us. Potatoes, carrots, onions and turnips were an important part of the Irish diet for centuries. These were all vegetables that grew within the earth and were nurtured by it. Up until fifty or sixty years ago, most people in rural Ireland still drank from local springs and wells. By eating and drinking of the earth, we become part of her and she becomes part of us. That is a relationship that the Irish know instinctively.

In Ireland, people will fight for ownership of the tiniest piece of land. It is said that Irish emigrants threw out food, to put soil in their pockets, because they knew that they would never see this land again. That ache for the land is deep within us. It is why people from the Americas and Australia come back generations later. We ache for the land because we have that relationship. This land is our mother.

Nothing is more important than taking conscious responsibility for the land on which we live, assisting that land in whatever way we can, by putting down seeds, talking to trees, maintaining old wells, or taking out rocks that impede the flow of a stream. That is all part of our responsibility to the land. We are conscious, we have the ability and we have the physical mobility to do that work.

We are here to be the guardians and stewards of the land and we should not forget that. We can get caught up in the twenty-first century but, if we spend a few days in and with nature, it brings us back to that realisation. I firmly believe that everybody needs to spend a week in nature at least once a year, just for their own wellbeing.

Plant Medicine

Many of us grew up with plant medicine because we lived in the countryside. There are plants around us for everything we need. That is part of their role and their gift to us. Our gift to them is to help protect them in certain weathers and to give them fertiliser or whatever they need to grow stronger.

All plants hold their own very specific medicine. We have had herbal medicine since the beginning of time. Modern day medicine is based on herbal medicine. Nowadays, they recommend chemical medicine, because there is more money to be made from it, but plant medicine is more natural to us.

In many tribal traditions, the medicine person or shaman journeyed into the person's energy field to see what entities were there and why they were causing illness. Plants have entities and most can assist us to bring balance. They can come and fight those entities that are making us unwell. Some tribal traditions actually visualise it that way. In this part of the world, we no longer see it like that, but I know of healers who still work with plant medicine in that way. They call on the entity of plants and they make their herbal remedies and their remedies are strong because of that. Some healers call upon Airmid, who was the herbal healer of the Tuath Dé.

To make herbal remedies, we can journey to the plant and to the being of that plant and ask it to assist us with the work we are doing. We ask for permission to take some of the leaves, or to dig up one of their roots because we need to make medicine with it. That makes the medicine very potent.

Elements and Elementals

The Middle World is this reality with all the magic still held within it. Since the time of Christianity, there has been a systematic effort to rid the world of magic and to regard our more ancient deities as evil and against life. Now, as a people, we are opening again to the awareness of the presences that share this living space with us – all those seen and unseen, betwixt and between.

The four elements – fire, earth, air and water are an essential part of our Middle World and vital for our lives. We have also seen their place on the Wheel. The elements of fire, earth, air and water are also used in many shamanic rituals and in shamanic healing.

There are elementals associated with each of the elements.

> **Fire** – fire sprites and dragons

> **Earth** – dwarfs, leprechauns and others

> **Air** – elves, fairies and other air sprites

> **Water** – the mer-people.

These magical creatures belong in most cultures in the world, although they may be called by different names.

The fairy folk are a rich part of our tradition in Ireland. Our whole culture is peppered with stories of the fairies. When I was growing up, all of the old people believed in them. My granny encouraged us to put out bread and butter and sugar sandwiches for them. Fairies came to me as a child and have been part of my world since.

There are many types of elementals which seem to be classified as 'fairies' nowadays. The fairies I played with when I was young were tiny, light-filled elementals. I could only see their shapes when they were not moving much (although, looking back, they seemed in constant motion). Their bodies were long, in relation to their width, and there was always a group of them, rather than one or two. I played with them in a tunnel that is still here, beneath the hill where I live. Now, it has been closed down by local farmers, for fear of children falling in or sheep getting stuck. It was always dark in the tunnel until the fairies came to join me. My older cousin still remembers me taking him down there and the lights coming, fluttering, towards us. He ran off quickly while I, of course, stayed.

After the conference in Killarney, where I took my first group of women on pilgrimage, my then husband came over and brought my two youngest children, aged seven and five. I was telling him about taking the women out and that some of them had seen small, light-filled fairies. My daughter asked me what fairies looked like. So, I brought them to Torc Waterfall which is strong in fairy energy and said, "Look over there and just allow your hearts to open. Allow all the love you feel to flow out through you and just wait."

My husband was standing opposite me, at the other side of the children. A fairy came down and flew around my daughter's head and face. It had a tiny body with glimmering, gossamer wings and was earth coloured, rather than multi-coloured. When it moved, it was like a light moving swiftly. It flew down to my son and then flew away. The children asked quietly, "What do we do?"

"You have to leave her a gift. Either you leave a spit or a wee or a little bit of your hair. You leave her something of yourself." The two of them pulled at their hair and put some down for the fairy. As they did, a large gathering of about thirty fairies flew over in front of them. I looked at my husband and he was crying, because he had never seen fairies before either.

When we got back to the house I asked the children to draw what they had seen. On the back of each page, I put their name and the date because I knew that when they were older, I would tell them and they would say, "Oh, Mum, that's just one of your stories".

To this day I can say to my daughter, "Do you remember?" And she says "Yes, I do". It is wonderful that she remembers that magic that fed her.

The whole multiverse, from the greatest galaxy to the smallest atom, is going through an evolutionary phase. Every single vibration, every level of being is evolving at the same time as we are. The earth, the universe, and then the other realm, the elementals, are also evolving. Up until now, the fairies did the work that they did, to enrich and beautify nature. Now, they have a choice whether to work with us or not and I have seen places that have lost the fairy energy.

Some years ago, a friend rang and said, "Amantha, the fairies have gone from Derrynane. We've got to do something." I rang another friend and we arranged to go there. On the way, we stopped in a place that has powerful fairy energy. We attuned, asked them if they would help us and if they would come with us where we were going. With two other friends, we went to Derrynane and walked into the woods. We called upon them and asked the fairies, from where we had been, to come and work with us in this place. And we started singing, sounding, dancing and energising the place again, dreaming them there again, and feeling the delight of the energy that they bring. When it felt complete, we left them gifts of chocolate, among other things.

About three weeks later, the phone rang and it was a woman whom I know well.

"Amantha, I was down in Derrynane and all the fairies are back. It's amazing, the whole place is filled with fairies." This woman knew nothing about what we had done!

Nowadays, fairies have a choice whether to work with us or not, so it is our role to call to them and bring them back again to work with us and with nature around us.

It is beautiful to bring that magic into our lives and to remember that we have that magic, that magic-nation, lying there within us. It is there when we perceive with our third eye, rather than our physical eyes. Sometimes we get so caught up with life that we forget what is real, because society, politically, economically, religiously, does not want us to remember. We must not be naïve. They do not want us to be fully empowered. Yet, despite everything, we are breaking through that projection that is being put upon us and we are seeing.

Tree Medicine

In the ancient stories, Ireland was once peopled by trees and stones that could speak to each other. The trees had legs and they walked, not in the same way we walk, and not as quickly, but they could move. We have always had a deep relationship with trees and I believe it was the same for all indigenous peoples. As each new people arrived in the country, they had to make a relationship with the trees as a way of surviving on the land. Some archaeologists now suspect that trees may have been an important part of our ancient sites.

Our first calendar was a thirteen-month, tree calendar in which each movement was a different tree. Each of our native trees has its own meaning, mystical and medical, and its own *ogham* symbol. We can use some parts of certain trees and not others because they might be poisonous to humans.

Just as we can journey to our ancestors, to the fairy and spirit realms, we can also journey to the trees and feel their presence. We can feel when they start to go into slumber, when they sleep, when they begin to waken and when they open their branches. Seeing them in nature, we can be with them on their cycle. Their cycle can teach us about our own rhythms in life. The presence of the trees is powerful and can hold us. We can find which tree is ours.

There can be guardian trees by certain megalithic or sacred sites. In forests and woods, there can be one or two trees that are guardian trees to all the rest. They hold that space and we should ask their permission to be there and to work in that area. Trees can also be our guardians.

Stone People

In my tradition, we also have the Stone People. Stones are deep, deep vibrations of energy and are connected to the earth. They can harmonise, hum and can draw energy down through the multiverses into the earth. By connecting with other stones, they can weave wonderful networks. Stones have deep power and deep knowing. If the Stone People like us, they will show us a face – we will see a face in the stone.

Some, but not all stones, can be storytellers. They are the keepers of the stories. The stones are the bones of the body of the earth. Just as the bones of our bodies hold stories, so too do the stones. When we attune to them, the stones can share those stories with us

Our ancient ancestors, going back eight thousand years or more, spent generations building ancient monuments that still stand today. It could take up to fifty generations to build one of these sites. We know now that those people came in from the West and the great graveyard of Carrowmore, in County Sligo, was one of the first sites to be built. Over centuries, they moved very slowly eastwards, working on Carrowkeel, then Loughcrew and finally the great ritualistic site of Brú na Bóinne – Newgrange, Knowth and Dowth. These structures were aligned with the movements of the sun and moon and with certain turnings of the Wheel, for example the winter solstice. The rising sun of the winter solstice comes through the lintel box at Newgrange. They know now that the Samhain sunrise goes into the main megalithic tomb in Carrowmore.

These early people drew hieroglyphs on the stones at those sites, from the basic cup marks, ring marks and zig-zags, to spirals, sun-like symbols, the eight spoked wheel and the famous triple spiral. The meaning of those hieroglyphs is open to interpretation. Many of them are similar to hieroglyphs found on stones in sacred places in France, Brittany, Portugal and Spain, but it is thought that the triple spiral is unique to Ireland. I, personally, find it very powerful to journey with some of these symbols.

A stone can last for millennia and it can hold energy. People come and go, but the stones stay to remind us of what is important in our life, who we are and what is important to our people. If we can connect with that, we can also find the sacred, because those stones were sacred. Some of those ancient sites held bodies, others were places of ritual. Our people still placed bodies in those tombs, thousands of years after the sites were built. In Carrowkeel, they found the bodies of babies from the time of the famine. Because these babies were not baptised in the Catholic tradition, it was believed that they would go to limbo rather than heaven. It is thought that those people in famine times went back to the older sites in the hope that the older gods or goddesses would help them.

Dolmen stones can often be guardian stones to a stone circle and they can become portals through which we can move into the space of betwixt and between. We can move into what happened there before. They can open our consciousness to be able to shapeshift into another space and time. I have, personally, retrieved much information through working in this way.

Crystals have come back into the consciousness of humanity since the 1980s. Before that, they were almost forgotten by most people. They were used in Egyptian times. Many of the native peoples always worked with crystals.

Around Ireland, we have grottoes with statues of Mary. Many of them are built on rocks containing quartz crystal. Perhaps unconsciously, people built them in those places because crystals have a reputation for magnifying things and prayers said in those places are magnified.

We can programme some crystals. Others have their own force and are too powerful for us to programme. They already have an internal programme. Those crystals come to us rather than us choosing them, because they know that we can work with them for the enhancement of the earth.

Symbolic Reflections

Power Objects

Power objects are any objects to which we give power, or objects that already have power with which we can work. In the Christian Church, the cross is an example of a power object. It is widely used and recognised and signifies something specific. The chalice is also a power object that goes back before Christianity. Throughout time, it has been used as a symbol of the womb.

We might have an object that means something to us, something that we picked up on our travels or in a place that is sacred to us. It could be a stone, crystal, feather, carving, symbol, or any object that we feel holds power. Before we work with that object, we should ask permission. Do you want to come with me? Can we work together? Just because we are attracted to it does not mean that it is for us (just as we could be attracted to a person who is completely the wrong person for us). It could be meant for somebody else or could be working on something completely different.

By asking permission, we open communication and connect with the object. Then we find, or feel, what that object wants to work with. We journey into it. What do we feel drawn to with it? Where is it taking us? What does it want of us?

Often, I visualise the crystal, stone or object as being the size of a castle or a tall house and I open the door, go inside and feel the energies in all the aspects of this house. I see if it is meant to be here and ask if we are meant to work together. Sometimes the energy is very strong. We can love this object, but if we feel that we get lost in its energy, then it is not necessarily ours to have or to work with. If we feel that we are imposing on it, or if it is pulling energy from us, then that is not what is meant to be. We are meant to hold our own integrity.

Any object can become a power object if we put intention into it. Even a piece of glass, if we continually put intention into it, becomes a power object.

Divination

Throughout the world, people have always used tools for divination. Divining is a way of reading the markings, to aid or support people. They used bones, sticks, stones and anything of that nature.

Divination is using something outside of yourself as a reflection for getting to know what you know within yourself. If you cannot tap into it within yourself, you can use tools to reflect that back to you. Some examples of divination in Ireland are: crystals, bones, playing-card readings, dowsing (there was an old man in north Kerry who did water divining for the County Council), palmistry, birth charts, *ogham* and reading tea leaves. My Auntie May, (Granny's daughter) used tea leaves, playing cards and palmistry.

The first written language we had in Ireland was *ogham* which is a tree language. It is made up of groups of horizontal markings on a vertical line, writing from the bottom upwards and is normally inscribed on a curve or corner, rather than on a flat plane. These markings were originally left on trees, by our early medicine people (now called druids) as a way of sharing information with each other. Later, the Celts, were enamoured with our tree language and used it on stones for burial sites, land markings and other purposes.

Some people use *ogham* for divination. They make sticks from the bark or twigs of native trees and make *ogham* markings on them. The *ogham* tree language has its own mythology and magic, so they are good tools for a reading.

The most important thing to remember with divination is that the person who reads it will be given the information that comes up for them to read. If I see the nine of swords as a certain thing, and that is what needs to be told to that person, that tarot card will come for me to tell them that. It might mean something different to them, if they were to read it for themselves.

Connection Tools

Totems and Allies

A totem is a helper who is with us on a long-term basis, for anything from five years to a lifetime. An ally is normally a helper who comes in and out. Fox could be an ally who is with us just for today to help us to see something. Tomorrow, it might be eagle, crow, beetle, or mouse. We may notice these animals in our everyday lives or experience them as symbols in times of danger or transition. They also accompany us on shamanic journeys. Knowing our totems and recognising our allies strengthens us and allows us to access information which can assist us, or the people around us, in times of need.

There are times when we need to come down into ourselves and be aware of the animal self. At other times, we need to stretch up and recognise the human self. How often do we allow ourselves to fall into the animal, the reactive, rather than bringing ourselves out into the human?

When we get used to working with our totems, it can be a good exercise, for a while, to start recognising the animal in other people. What animal is that? We can look at the way they act and talk and can see that this person is a beaver, or that person is a cow. That may have many meanings. The cow is considered sacred and is connected to the Mother because of the milk that it gives us. Every part of the cow can be used by us. It also has a little stump on its forehead where they say, in mythology, that it once had a horn, like a unicorn's. The cow is also connected to the star system of the Pleiades, the seven sisters, the seven muses. There is sacredness around the cow.

It is important to remember that the helpers are not only from the animal realm, they can also be from the elemental realm. We could have a leprechaun, fairy, dragon or mer-person as a helper.

Grandmothers' Circle

I was lucky to grow up with a grandmother whom I adored. Everybody loved her. Even friends that I brought back to Kerry called her 'Granny'. At night, women came and sat around the fire: Kitty Mannix, Cissie Broderick and Hannah, sometimes Maggie Mannix and occasionally Eilis. There was Mrs Leary whom we called 'Big Granny'. She and my granny had been friends since they were children and she was as tall as my granny was tiny. So my granny was 'Small Granny' and she was 'Big Granny'. They sat around the fire in the evenings and told stories. I could not learn from books, but I never forgot what they talked about and shared. These elder women were my first grandmother circle. When the women left there, they were settled – even one of them who was an unsettled woman.

From then, that knowing of a grandmothers' circle was instinctive in me. Whenever a group of us got together, I felt a circle of grandmothers around us. When I started with the woman's group in my early thirties, they were very strongly there. In the first two groups I had, there was often a vacant chair in the circle. We all acknowledged it without doing anything about it. It always felt as if there was somebody sitting there and that it was a grandmother. I could feel the presence of one and, often, another grandmother who came to support me. There was one Australian aboriginal grandmother who came to me a lot. I could never understand why, because I had no Australian blood, no connection with Australia and no sense that I needed to go there or had a life there in another time. Yet, the aboriginal grandmother was a very strong presence. Over time, I began to recognise this circle of grandmothers and that each of them came from a different place; they had different skin, different eyes, different hair, yet they were all part of this circle. I also feel that, when my granny passed over, she became part of that circle. Every time we gather together, even in my groups that include men, I am conscious of the presence of the grandmother circle. The grandmothers are here to remind us of what we carry.

Traditionally the grandmothers were the holders of the stories. We always think of the Cailleach, the old woman, the hag, the crone, the grandmother holding that wisdom. Much of that knowledge has been forgotten or suppressed by patriarchal society, or by religions. That information is still there within us. All we have to do is retrieve it.

I truly believe that, whenever a group of women gathers together, the circle of grandmothers comes to them. The grandmothers and their grandmothers and their grandmothers, a spiral of foremothers going away back, are there now to help us to retrieve all the knowing of who we are as women. The deep magic and mystery within us is powerful beyond anything. We need to reclaim that and be in balance with ourselves and with life, so that we can be here for our great Mother Earth. I do not mean this as a way of putting men down. We women are just reclaiming what is ours, which should never have been taken, forbidden or forgotten. So we are re-membering, reweaving ourselves back into that knowing again. That brings us into a better place with a man because we meet as equal and other.

Personal Story

Every person has a story and is a story. Our bodies show that story. We need to honour each person for carrying their story and for being their story.

At some point, each of us needs to tell our story, whether we tell it to our children or to friends. Telling our story is a powerful process and very therapeutic. Some people feel so much pressure to tell their story that they need to go away somewhere to do it.

Many elders feel the need to share their stories with us. They instinctively know that they need to share their stories before they pass over. When I visit my aunt she delights in telling me the stories of my people. I love listening, because she is the last of that generation and I know that when she is gone, all of those stories will be gone too. She tells me things that my grandchildren, and even my own children, would not believe because we have gone through such times of transition since my aunt was a young girl.

Prayer

The Irish have always been a prayerful and soulful people whose interrelationship with nature and life all around them is evident in their continuous blessings and prayers which have carried the people throughout time. Before the coming of Christianity, the wells and springs were dedicated to female deities. People, often women, gathered at the wells and called upon the deity to fill their bowls and containers with the life-giving force of water.

"St Patrick's Breastplate", a prayer from early Christian times, has been used continuously through the generations and has survived to this day. *Anam Cara,* a spiritual book by John O'Donoghue, Irish poet and mystic, contains many authentic Irish prayers and blessings which were passed down from ancient times.

The power of prayer is huge, when people come together, focus and hold their intention, even for five minutes.

It is powerful to sit and pray as a community and then we have to live it. That is what I call active prayer. As a people, we need to actively engage with consciousness, love, intelligence and awareness, for the good of the earth. Otherwise, people will act without consciousness or awareness, to the detriment of the earth. We need to do that as an active prayer.

Every time we cross a stream, we can bless the water. By the sea, we can send blessings of light and harmony out into the water, so that they can carry all across the world.

Dreaming

Dreams and Visions

When Granny and the other women shared stories, I would go into the dream of those stories. I would meet those beings, Medb, Brigit, Fionn McCool and Cúchulainn. The stories awaken our ability to be part of the dream world. In the Irish tradition, dreaming was practised by the *fílí,* the poets. It is part of the old way of accessing information that lies within the recesses of our consciousness and within the presence of life around us. We can bring that information through dreaming, through words, through song or through music.

Irish people are very visual. I have learnt that through working with people from different cultures. The Irish have a great ability to see inwardly, whereas a lot of other people feel or sense things. In Ireland, nearly everybody has the ability to see within, to close their eyes and visualise. It seems to be part of our nature. Ireland herself is a little betwixt and between as a country. That is why the stories are so strong here and why we have held the sacred sites. To this day, very few people will cut down fairy forts, because there is an understanding that we have another realm that we no longer physically see. That is particular to us as a people. We have fought for hundreds upon hundreds of years to keep that. We fought not just for our land and our Christian beliefs but for all of our indigenous beliefs, so as a people, we have been able to hold that way of dreaming. It connects us to other indigenous peoples.

Dreaming True

We can use our ability to dream to manifest what we need in life. We call this process dreaming true. The dream body is connected to the womb area and the throat. For women, especially, the womb is our place of creativity. It is there that we create, not just children of the body but children of the mind. It is also where we work on our level of intention.

Energetically, the vibratory field that we use to create, comes through the womb area and out through the throat. Those two chakras, working together, bring creativity into motion.

The womb holds our idea, thought or venture and it is where we nurture and feed it. When we seek to create something, we see it, clarify it, hold it in our intention and, then, we give it sound. We allow that sound to flow through our throats. It does not come from the throat itself. The sound comes from the womb and up through the throat. That gives our intention a body, a vibratory field that magnifies the attraction a hundredfold.

According to some ancient teachings, the world is built on sound and we are all made up of sound frequencies. In the beginning was the word. Sound is vibration and vibration attracts and creates form. Every living thing has sound: every blade of grass, leaf, bird, deer, fish and spider. We respond to sound.

We hold our intention in the womb and, by giving it sound, we give it a body. As we release the sound, we put it out into the etheric field, so we move the creativity up, out of the womb and into the universe to attract back to us. In some very old stone paintings, there were images of babies coming out of the mouth. We all know that is impossible, but those babies symbolised the sound, the creativity coming through the throat.

As often as we can during the day we visualise, in our mind's eye, what we want to create. Then, we give it sound. Even if we have little time available to us, I highly recommend that, whether we are using the toilet or waiting for the kettle to boil, we take a few seconds to close our eyes and see what we seek to attract. We see it in its entirety and hold the vision. Once we clearly see what we want, we can attract it into the here and now. Every time we sit and focus on the dream that we seek to bring into reality, we give it a sound vibration, so we are creating a form for that dream. The more often we do that the quicker it will manifest in our lives.

As well as focusing on our intention and giving it sound, we need to engage in creative thinking. There is a difference between creative and positive thinking. Positive thought is where we hold the thought but do nothing about it. We sit back and wait for it to come to us. Creative thought involves action. We visualise what we want, then move towards it by planting the seeds, watering them, fertilising them and nurturing that which we are creating.

I remember a woman saying to me once, "I don't believe in astrology any more. My chart said I was going to meet the man of my dreams in November, and I never did."

"What did you do?" I asked her.

"What do you mean?"

"What did you do to meet that man? What did you do the first weekend?"

"I was cleaning my house," she said.

"So you never went outside? You never went dancing or partying?" I enquired.

"No."

"Well, he's probably still out there looking for you!" I said. "How are you going to find him? You've got to do some work too!"

When we start to create, our wombs bring that magic. It is important to allow ourselves to create and to know we have that ability. We can look back on things we have done in our lives. Whether it was a child, a drum or a beautiful home, we created it. We all know how to create and we can do it because we have done it before.

Sharing Dreams

Sometimes we need someone to share our dream and other times we need to dream it for ourselves. Especially in relationships, there are men who want women to share and help them to cultivate their dreams. As women, we have the ability to hold dreams. We are the creatrixes. Because of that, a man will almost always need a woman with or behind him when he wants to create. Women need to be clear about whether that is part of their dream. It is wonderful when a couple shares a dream together. There are times when the dream might belong to him and not to her. Whatever relationship we are in, it is important to recognise if we share the same dream. Two people could be dreaming very different dreams and not realise it. We need to be sure that we do not carry someone else's dream instead of our own.

Some people really support us in our dreams. They dream with us, so they strengthen that dream. That helps us to attract it more easily.

There are people with whom it is not good to share our dreams. They say, "Sure, what would you do with that, for God's sake? When are you going to get time to do that?" That shatters something that we are beginning to build up and that affects us. They are not the person to share our dreams.

Lending our energy into somebody's dream is very powerful, although we have to be quite clear whether that is part of our dream or not. If it is not our dream, it can drain us. Sometimes, other people's dreams can inspire us. They can make us say, "Oh, yes! That's fantastic." Then, the healthy thing to do is to go away and ask ourselves, "Is that my dream? I can really see how inspiring that is for them, but is it mine?"

If we do not have our own dream, there is a danger that other people will create our reality for us, or that we will get swallowed up in their dreams. It is important that we consciously create our own reality, otherwise we may find ourselves at the mercy of others.

Sound and Movement

Drumming and Chanting

Traditionally, every indigenous people of the world used drumming as a way of accessing the other realm and calling on spirits. In Ireland we use the *bodhrán*. It is a way of saying: "Wake up! Come join us!" Drums can waken up that energy around us and layers within us that have gone to sleep.

Many years ago, when I journeyed with Tlachtga, on the Hill of the Ward, the words came to me. "Hush, shhh, hear the pulse of her nature. Listen, sisters, to the beat of her heart." Tlachtga gifted me the ability to hear the heartbeat of the Mother. That heartbeat was very important as a way of accessing information in the Lower World. Then I used the *bodhrán* to beat the heartbeat of the Mother. Because realities began shifting in me when I worked with that beat, I started using it for journeying.

The drum is used as an accompaniment for shamanic journeying and for rituals and rites of passage. It can be used for walking the wheel, although I find that a rattle is better for journeying to the deities.

Sometimes the drum is used to bring people into a trance, so that they move into an altered state from where they can pick up information. We all have the ability to open to that information, but we often do not believe that we can do that and so, we limit ourselves.

I also use the drum to read rips and holes in the energy body of someone who comes to me for healing. That is my teaching. Beating the drum, the drum showed me how to do that. You build a relationship with your drum. The skin of the Irish drum is the goat. The frame of the drum is a hardwood. You walk a while with the goat, thanking it for giving you the skin. Every time you take it out of the bag you rub it really hard, especially if your hands are sweaty, that is the best oil for the drum. You and the drum are not separate; when there is a relationship, the drum will tell you things. If there is somebody there, the drum tells me. Especially when I do house clearing, the drum tells me if there is something not in alignment. The drum changes tone and feeds that back to me.

Every single living thing has sound – a vibration, a frequency. Every part of your body is the harmonic of one frequency, one note. If you cut that note, you can hear the harmonics and hear if one part is out of harmony. The drum reflects that back to you.

The drum is feminine. It is round and symbolises the womb. The beater symbolises the penis as it awakens the sound, just as the penis is supposed to awaken a woman's passion and sexual energy. There is a whole sensual energy around the drum. When we drum, we awaken our creativity which sits in our womb area, whether we still physically have a womb or not.

The earth has a heartbeat. Just as the foetal heartbeat is faster than the mother's, so our heartbeat is faster than the earth's. The drum also symbolises the Mother's heartbeat. If we play our drum with our hand, we can find that heartbeat. There will be a place on our drum where the sound is just perfect.

When I am drumming, I find that I can hear when the spirits and the ancestors begin to move in. It is as if there is another tone underneath my drum, as if they are singing. In a group in Madison,

Wisconsin a few of the participants heard a violin. They thought that I had put background music on for the journey. It was the drum calling on the energies and the energies responding. The drumbeat, working with the energies of the ancestors that were there, created that sound.

We can drum together to bring balance and cohesion into a group. While drumming, we have to keep rhythm with everyone else and that unites us. We weave in and out when we are drumming. Our energies begin to form. So it begins to shift and move us.

If we each begin drumming our own beat, even though it is different, we all end up harmonising together. We become harmonics of the one sound. That happens naturally. It comes to a point where we are all together. Energetically, that is what we do in a group or in a circle. We all come in from our own space carrying whatever we are carrying and, gradually, we become the one energy and we merge. That is a great gift.

Another way to bring cohesion into a group is through chanting. Women love chanting. We were born for it. It unites us. Chants are also used during rituals and rites of passage.

Trance Dance and Shapeshifting

When we put on music and allow our bodies to move, we can let go of the confines of our minds and emotions and simply be in the presence of energy. There, we can embrace all that we are.

For me the music of Sliabh Luachra (on the borders of Kerry, around The Paps) has strong strains of the Tuatha Dé Danann music which, it is said, could make people laugh, cry or sleep. Irish music evokes emotions and energies through us. Really good *sean nós* singing (traditional songs, often sung by women) can take us into other zones. It is not as common now as it was, but they can bring us into places within the recesses of our own psyche, to bring forth what we did not know we held.

Irish dancing changed a lot through the centuries, particularly since 1923 when dancers were not allowed to kick their legs up and dancing became very straight and only from the knees downwards. In the ancient stories of Bealtaine, the young people danced and sang and then went off to make love. The dancing and singing brought them to that level. We do not know how they danced, but we have the Kerry Polka, which is fast and twirling and we can see how easily we can move into trance through that.

Consciously breathing in and out, relaxing into the beat of the music, we can call our totems and allies to join us in the dance. As we relax into the music itself, we allow our totems to merge with us. When we call upon and merge with our animal self, we merge with a deep, integral part of our nature that knows how to move with the beat and that breathes with the rhythm of life itself. The more we merge with our animals, the more we can recognise those aspects of them in us, allowing us to embrace them in a coherent, loving way. In that space we can be all of who and what we are. Embracing our animal nature gifts us the opportunity to integrate parts of ourselves that we might fear.

Trance dance is just one form of shapeshifting. Another is to envisage ourselves as the teacher, writer, singer or artist that we want to be and to shapeshift into that. When we envisage it, we give our subconscious the opportunity to feel, or see, ourselves as that, allowing ourselves to move more easily into that role. Sometimes, without realising it, we can shapeshift into other realities. We need to be aware of keeping the integrity of our human body intact, if we choose to move into other realities.

Throughout time, medicine people in indigenous tribes have worked with shapeshifting. Energetic shapeshifting is used in some forms of healing. If somebody is unconscious or very ill, we can shapeshift through their energy field to see what is occurring. Then we shapeshift back into our own integrity, bringing back the information that is needed to assist that person.

Soul Work

Entities/Extractions

Occasionally we meet someone and feel a very strange energy from them. They can have what I term 'company', meaning that they have entities around or attached to them.

Entities are energies that get caught in a person's energy field. Sometimes thought forms can be entities that are floating around and, because we have a weakness or propensity towards those thoughts, we allow them to get stuck in our energy field. "Poor me" syndrome is a common entity.

Another example, prevalent in Ireland, is alcoholism. An alcoholic will attract entities, often from other alcoholics who have passed over and whose entities look for another host. When we walk into some bars, we can feel the energy, although we do not know what it is. If an alcoholic walks in and feels that energy, he will have a sense that this is a good place and the entities who have lived in other alcoholics will find a home in him. Entities can be picked up by other people with addictions to drugs, food or emotions.

Entities try to feed off our energy and they always need to be extracted. In this lifetime we are meant to become empowered beings in a human form, so we do not give our bodies up for another to come through. That weakens us and takes from all that we can be. There is no essence of light that would take over our bodies without our permission, so any entity that takes us over in that way is essentially negative and needs to be extracted.

It is different when we work shamanically and engage with specific entities for specific work. I call upon Tlachtga to work with me when somebody is dying, or I called upon Brigit to help me with the birth of my granddaughter. That is a relationship with the entity, not being taken over by it.

Extractions can be tied into soul retrieval. When we sing the soul home, sometimes we have to release the energies that may have caused it to stay separate. We work with the person to release that, so that they can take in all that they are without taking in the fear, memory and shock that is tied around it. That is one form of extraction.

We need to do extractions when something is not in alignment with the person's energy field, not in harmony with their weave, or when something is not supportive of their life's growth and the unfolding of their being upon their path.

As a practitioner, if I work with a person, clearing their bodies, using a feather, drum or rattle, I might find something that is not in alignment with their body. The first thing I do is ask their permission, so that I move from personal (what I think I should be doing) to impersonal (what is meant to be done for that person). It is not what I believe or think, but what is right and necessary for that person.

I tell the person that there is something that is not in alignment and I ask them how they feel about me working with that. If they give me permission, I start working with them to remove it. I might ask: "If I ask you to place your hand on your left breast, what comes to your mind?" As they start speaking, the feather changes or the sound of the rattle or drum starts to change. The person participates in the process. As they release it, I also extract it.

Sometimes I journey into and around the person's weave because there are things trying to get in. If you see images of blood cells under the microscope, there can be little things attacking the cells and trying to break them down. Something similar can happen around someone's weave. That can be other people's negativity towards that person, or it can be something that they picked up.

Sometimes extractions can be needed for negative thoughts and not just for our own negative thoughts about ourselves. There may be somebody who is very negative about us and, if they know how to use that energy consciously, that can affect us. That is not an entity, but a thought pattern that needs extracting.

An unhealthy thought can become an unhealthy weakness either on us, in us or somewhere else, if we are the ones directing it. Most people direct those thoughts consciously to harm us. Others do it unconsciously. They are not aware that they are doing it, but they exert power over us. If we said to them, "You are actually causing that person a weakness by your negative focus of attention on them", they might be quite shocked.

It is not healthy to send our negative intentions to people we dislike. Instead of harbouring negative thoughts, we have to be very clear about what is right for us and for those around us and live our lives accordingly. It is best to focus on change and how to implement that, rather than losing energy by getting caught up in that negativity. We can align ourselves with others who understand and live by what is right. That is the better way to bring change.

House and Land Clearing

People leave imprints. If people have lived in disharmony, anger or pain, a house can hold that energy. An imprint can be left in the energy field of the house or the land. It is similar to putting your hand in something and making an imprint on the wall.

Some people who buy houses feel the energy there. People may live for many years with something not being right. A shamanic practitioner can feel that ghostly energy. Sometimes we need to journey into it and, if there is a negative or difficult entity there, it needs to be cleared. If it is an energy that has been left behind, we can clear that.

I have done a lot of house clearing. The tools I use are fire, candles, or, sometimes, lavender and salt. Traditionally, in Ireland, lavender was grown outside as a protection for the house. The smell and colour invoke good energies. I also use a drum and, sometimes, rattles. Using those tools, I start at the front door and work my way through every opening of every room, every window, corner and fireplace, drumming through it all, clearing it and bringing in the light. I call upon the light to help me to release what is there. I also open the window and let it out.

One woman asked me to come because her two young boys were not sleeping at night and ended up in her bed because they were frightened in their room. As I went into the boys' room, I felt a sudden tiredness, as if I had been hit backwards. I put down the drum, sat cross-legged on one of the beds, and went into the energy to see what it was. There was a vortex and I closed it and cleared the energy. It took me at least an hour just in that room and then I cleared the rest. When I do that work, I get very cold, no matter how warm the day is. From that night onwards, the boys slept right through until morning. Those little boys knew nothing of what I had done, yet the energy in their room had changed and they could feel it.

Depending on what has happened on the land, there can be imprints left of that too. If there were battles, especially where people died slowly over a few days, that energy can transmit itself into the land. The land does not forget. She will forgive, although she will hold the story. It is Her-story.

In Ireland we can have sadness in the land. There are fields where people were buried during the famine and people have forgotten. Their energy may have seeped into the land. It is important to honour that energy and recognise that. As children, we were told about fields near Scartaglen and warned never to go there at night. There were stories that young people went into those fields and tried to cross them at night, but could not find their way out. One man had a few drinks, crossed the field and could not find his way out. Next morning, he woke beside the gate. He had spent the whole night thinking he could get nothing to eat or drink. That energy was there in the land.

When someone builds a house, they need to walk on the land first and tune in. How does the land feel about this? What is it holding? Is it going to be productive? If they intend to have children, they need to ask if this is a healthy energy for their children to grow up with. People need to be aware. If there are energies that are not healthy, they need someone to work with them. I have worked with places and with people who would normally never dream of asking somebody like me to come and work with them.

Clearing our own houses, using lavender or smouldering sage, is a good thing to do occasionally. It is like having a shower: it clears away that energy. When the women cleaned their houses in spring and built the fire up for Brigid, they put salt outside around the house. Salt is powerful and holds all of the elements within it. It comes from the sea, is washed up on the sand which is earth; it is dried by the sun which is fire and it is lifted by the air. Our tears are salt. And often when we cry we have a clearing.

Soul Retrieval and Cutting the Ties

Soul retrieval means retrieving parts of ourselves, of our souls, that are still caught within a situation. When we went into shock, or experienced terror, part of us found the experience too much to bear and stepped out. That part of us, as a five, twelve or twenty-year-old, is still there, holding its breath and living that experience. It is still alive in our subconscious.

Parts of our soul can also get stuck under anaesthesia, when we were not fully and wholly within our own essence of being.

It can feel as if there is an essential part of our being that is not connected with the rest of us. That sometimes brings weakness, physically, emotionally or psychically. If it is left, it can become a dis-ease in the body.

Shamanic healing can help with singing the soul home – gathering the parts that are not in alignment with the essence of the person. Occasionally, soul retrieval is needed for an ancestral pattern in the family, when an imbalance, sometimes seen as a curse, has come down through the family.

Nobody ever showed me how to do soul retrieval. I have never seen anyone else do that work, although people obviously do it all over the world. That energy and information is in the collective unconscious, in the weave, and it comes through in different ways. This practice came through to me through my healing work.

There was a woman who was not of her right mind and, when she was in pain, mentally and emotionally, she came to my grandmother. Granny used to say, "Ah sure, God help us, the woman had a hard life and she lost parts of herself". She was the only one who could ease that woman's pain. I do not know if Granny practiced soul retrieval with her, because it was a private thing.

When we have an experience that still holds us, or if we hold on to that experience, the thread between us and the weave is pulled taut. That takes energy from us and can begin to affect us and our organs. As long as that thread remains uncut, it keeps us in a place of reaction. We will continue to attract similar experiences into our lives, through other people and other situations, until we cut that tie ourselves, or are assisted in cutting it.

Once we cut the ties to those experiences or people, we can choose not to react to them and we no longer attract similar experiences into our lives. We will never lose the experiences but we will no longer be defined by them. Those experiences become part of our weave. We can refer to them, or choose to revisit them for our personal medicine, or to explain things to somebody else. Once the ties are cut, those experiences no longer take energy from us.

I do not recommend that people work with soul retrieval unless they have been adequately trained. An untrained person can easily take on some of the other person's imbalances while trying to balance them.

Soul Midwifery

In the Ancient Irish tradition there is a belief that the soul journeys on, often assisted by a bee, to Tír na nÓg, to await re-birth, while the spirit becomes part of nature around us and the body returns to the Great Mother – we are born of the womb and return to the tomb.

When our weave is completed and it is time to move on again, it is also time to begin releasing the ties that bind us and regrets that we might be carrying. Those ties are not just with others; they can be with specific memories, items of ownership, karmic ties and with the elements – fire, earth, air, water and also ether*.

The role of the shamanic soul midwife is to assist those who are preparing for their great passing/transition and also those who have

---

* Ether is the upper region of air beyond the clouds. It is lighter than air and is traditionally seen as the veil between this and other realms.

passed on and are still tied to the earth's plane for some reason or another. It is best to assist the living while they are still conscious, although it can still be of great assistance if the person is unconscious.

For those who have passed over and have not yet passed on, it can be beneficial to assist them in releasing what is holding them and preventing them from travelling on. The soul midwife may be able to assist the person by reassuring them that the soul continues as the body begins its process of breaking down.

Soul midwifery involves working within the realm of betwixt and between and people require shamanic training to learn techniques for protection while working in these realms.

THE CHAKRAS

Introduction to the Chakras

The chakras are energy points, vortexes in the human body. They are well known in indigenous cultures and are part of the mass consciousness. The ten chakras that I use were shown to me by the earth Herself, here in Ireland. She showed me that they always begin with the feet and the earth, which is a deep brown colour. The feet ground us in the earth. I was taken up through the colours and shown the thymus and the chakra above our crown chakra – the chakra of communion. It makes it very personal to my teachings, that they were accessed from the earth here, in this place.

1 Feet – Brown

In my tradition, the first chakra is the feet. The colour is brown, because of the cool, rich, brown soil. When we turn over a sod of earth anywhere in Ireland, it is brown. Our first chakra connects us deep into the earth, into our Great Mother and our most ancient ancestors.

We feel those roots and that energy going way down into the earth. If we are standing, it is best to bend our knees slightly, so that the energy moves better. If we stand straight, we put pressure on the lower back, but with knees slightly bent, we feel ourselves pushing down and the energy moving.

If we have problems visualising the brown of the feet chakra, it means that we have difficulty grounding. That is common sense. We need to stand on our feet, grounded in the here and now.

It is important that we feel those roots and that energy going deep down into the earth. As followers or practitioners of the Way of the Seabhean, we bring our teachings into our reality. We are opening to who we are. That is something we may have ached to do for many years. We need to take the energy that we feel, and the things to which we are connected, and root them way down into the earth.

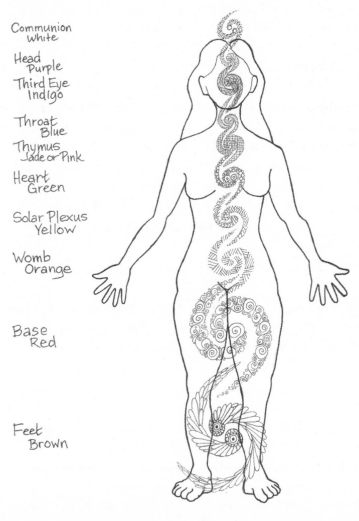

Communion
white

Head
Purple

Third Eye
Indigo

Throat
Blue

Thymus
Jade or Pink

Heart
Green

Solar Plexus
Yellow

Womb
Orange

Base
Red

Feet
Brown

Image by JoAnn Turner

2 Base – Red

Our second chakra is the base chakra, our tribal energy. The colour is red. It is raw power. We draw upon it to awaken power within us. Power is not good or bad in itself, it can be used well or abused. Power can include the power of love, service, nurturing or healing. We can draw upon that power, letting it flow through us. The image of the Indian snake charmer, playing his flute as the snake rises, is a very strong symbol for the base chakra, the kundalini energy. For me, it is a dragon rather than a snake. I love my fiery dragon and do not deny that energy; I draw it up and bring it out as my form of protection.

If we have difficulty visualising the red of the base chakra, it can either mean that we are still deeply embedded in our tribe, still manifesting aspects of the tribe rather than living in our own individuality, or it can mean that we have tried to cut off from the tribe and are not drawing upon the gifts of our ancestors or the roots coming up through us, to hold and feed us in this reality. To release patterns in our family, we need to be connected to our tribe. The best thing we can do to strengthen ourselves, is to see the gifts from the family and also see what has not supported or is not supporting us.

3 Womb – Orange

In my tradition, the third chakra is the womb, our chalice. The colour is orange and is to do with vitality. It is the place of a woman's personal power. There is nothing more powerful or magical than the ability to create life. Our womb is also our seat of creativity, where we create, not just children of the body but, children of the mind. Even if we do not have a womb, we still carry that energy.

As women, this is our own place of sacredness. It is the place where we go to be with our selves, to connect deep down. Quite often there is a fire there and we can sit with it. For some it is an orange cave.

This chakra, for men, is their scrotum, their seat of creativity. The power of the man is being able to instigate energy and protect space, so that the woman can do what she needs to do. In most of the animal realms, the male protects the female, holding that space so they can work and create together.

If we cannot see the orange colour, we may need to waken up our passion for life. Our creativity may be coming through our will, rather than from our womb area. We may be pushing our ideas on to someone else, instead of listening to their ideas and working with them, or we may not be accessing our own creative ability.

When we start to wake up that passion, we begin to awaken our sense of being alive. We realise that some things are not life-enhancing, but are drawing energy from us.

4 Solar Plexus – Yellow

The fourth chakra is the solar plexus, the colour yellow, like bile and sunlight and has to do with our instincts and emotions. Here, we become aware of what we feel by opening ourselves to honour that feeling and emotion and processing it.

That emotion might not be ours. If we ask, "What is this?" while breathing slowly and deeply, we can often see that we are picking this up from somebody else. Then we can release it. The words I use for this are: "This is not mine, I do not need it. This is not mine, I do not want it. This is not mine, I release it with love and light to go on its way."

If the emotion is ours, we need to claim it. We do not want to control it, but to observe it and be aware of what is going on within us. If someone makes us feel angry, we should not allow it to take us over or direct our anger on to them. Instead, we should own our reaction, gently and clearly letting the other person know that their behaviour is unacceptable.

If we have problems visualising the yellow of the solar plexus, it can mean that we have trouble with our emotions. We may be allowing our emotions to determine what we think. It could also indicate issues with our digestion.

Our solar plexus is also our animal nature which gives us signals as to whether a place or a person is safe. If our solar plexus screams that this place is not safe, we should recognise the message, thank our solar plexus and then check and see whether the place is actually unsafe, or whether we are picking up an imprint of negative energy that has been left there.

5 Heart – Green

Our fifth chakra is the heart and the colour is green. The heart is our personal love. Sometimes we hold people and things in our heart, things that we have lost: a home that we did not want to leave, for instance. If our heart aches, it can be because of something or someone that we are holding. We can also hold hurt that has been inflicted on us by those we love.

We need to be continually aware of breathing out and releasing things from the heart. If somebody is in need of love and pulling from us, this can interfere with our love and may also affect the health of the heart itself.

Sometimes, without realising it, we can close down our heart. There are times when our heart has to be broken to be broken into. Even though we have had great pain, it is a real teaching for us to allow the heart to stay open. If we allow the love to keep flowing through it, that keeps our heart healthier on the physical level too.

If we cannot see the colour green in this area, our hearts may be closed down, or we could be holding too much in our hearts. For example, if we have lost somebody whom we loved, we might have difficulty seeing green. If we see lots of green in this chakra, or if we continually wear green, that can mean that we are looking for space around us.

6 Thymus – Jade, Turquoise or Pink

The sixth chakra, the thymus, is located in the centre of the breastbone halfway between the heart and throat. Depending on who you are, the colour of the thymus chakra can be jade, turquoise or rose pink (the colour of rose quartz[*]). Also known as the high heart,[†] it is the chakra of unconditional, universal love. Unconditional love means never closing the love down, but allowing it to flow through continually and not denying another that love, even if they are somebody whom we dislike.

If we have difficulty visualising the colour of the thymus, we have problems with unconditional love and maybe with self-love in particular. We need to let love flow through us first to self. We need to recognise that we are worth all that love.

All it takes is for someone to frown at us and our thymus can close down. In the Catholic Church, we beat our breast saying, *"Mea culpa, mea culpa"* (through my fault I have sinned). That closes the thymus.

The thymus reacts very quickly to the environment around it. When it is open, it feeds the body with the T-cells it needs to fight disease. When it atrophies, the thymus does not feed the body all that it needs.

When we look in the mirror and smile, we can feel that love of self as a being in human form. If we smile at our reflection and say, "You look beautiful today", tapping on our thymus three times, we wake up the thymus and are filled with love for self. Through that, the love will flow to others.

7 Throat – Blue

The seventh chakra is the throat and the colour blue. It is the ability to speak our truth. When we speak in our true voice, we allow the energy to move up through us so that our vibration comes through, rather than from, the throat. Often we are afraid to speak in case we hurt other people's feelings. Yet, if we do not speak our truth, we

* For the Chinese and many other Asian cultures, the colour of the thymus is jade. Buddhists and Native Americans use turquoise for the thymus. New Age people, who are aware of the new energies, have rose quartz, the colour of unconditional love.

† I first heard this term used by a Lakota Sioux Native American medicine woman called Denise King Francisco who has become a dear sister. Denise gave me permission to use the name.

block our voice, our vibration.

When we want to create, we work with the throat and the womb together. We can speak our truth with love and allow it to be harmless. We do not have to speak our truth in such a way that it hurts another. Spirit said "truth, love and harmlessness", in that order. We speak our truth in a loving way without harming others. We also act with truth and love and act harmlessly. Living by that doctrine nourishes the throat and the throat area.

If we have difficulty seeing the colour blue of the throat chakra, we have difficulty or fear around speaking our truth. We might also have physical problems in the throat area.

Problems with the throat chakra can mean a closing down of our ability to give voice or sound. Most of us are born with the ability to give sound. It is a vibration that can attract and draw in the vibrations of others. If we do not give sound, we have trouble creating things and attracting things into our lives.

The colour blue is also connected to the family from which we originate. People who tend to wear a lot of blue are connected to their family. Traditionally, women dressed the men in blue, to keep the man in the family.

8 Third Eye – Indigo

The eighth chakra is our third eye, in the centre of our forehead, above the bridge of the nose. It is indigo, which is bluish purple, the colour of the ink we used at school. The third eye is our ability to see within and beyond.

When we use our third eye, we perceive something rather than looking at it. When we see someone begging, do we just see a beggar, or can we look within that to see another soul? The third eye allows us to see deeper.

When we see an image of something in our mind, we normally see only one part of it. If it is a horse, we might see the head, a part of the body or the tail swishing. If we step back energetically, we can see the entire horse. Taking another step back, we can see what is around it, a lake or trees. That is magic. It feels like our imagination, but imagination and magic can be the same thing.

If we have trouble visualising indigo, we could have closed down our third eye. We might not have wanted to see things unseen or unrecognised by others, or were fearful of seeing those things. We may have withdrawn or suppressed our ability to perceive. Sometimes, if the third eye is overused, it can cause headaches or stress on the body and the physical eyes.

9 Head – Purple

The head chakra is the colour purple. Some people see it like amethyst or slightly darker. It is communication and our ability to hear what is being said. One of the greatest gifts we can give another person is to see and hear them for who they are, without judgement. Then people can really be there with us. Sometimes the greatest healing and the greatest communication is had when sitting with another and just being, without words and with no words needed.

Our minds are not us. We are greater than our thoughts. When we wake in the morning, we can lie there and listen to our minds. We can change or still our minds. Therefore we are greater than them. The mind is like an animal that has not been trained. If we have been brought up in a country where the focus of education is on the mind only, then our minds have been overactivated and cultivated, so are difficult to still. One of the ways to still the mind is to give ourselves a visualisation. When we do that, we bring the mind into the place where we want it to be and hold it there. If we find it drifting off, we can bring it gently back.

If we cannot see purple, then we are not bringing the chakra energy up into the intellect. In that case, we are allowing our emotions to rule us. If the purple is extremely strong, then we can be too rational.

The mind can be the slayer or the illuminator of the real. Some people get stuck within a mind frame and never come out of it. Others can use their minds to open themselves to new ideas, to move beyond the mind into higher or super consciousness.

10 Communion – White

The tenth chakra is the chakra of communion and is above the head. The colour is white light. It is the energy of being at one with everything. As the first chakra, the feet, was the roots and the Lower World, the chakra of communion is the Upper World. We move into the place of being at one with spirit, being at one with the essence and divinity, being in that place of pure light and pure being. When we work through the chakras, starting from the feet and working up, by the time we reach that place, we find that we are at one. We do not need to think; we simply rest. It is like lying in white sunlight and feeling at one with all of life, feeling the presence of pure being.

If we balance all of the physical chakras in our bodies, then I have never known anybody to have a problem with the white light. Once our physical bodies are in harmony with themselves, then the energy, the harmonious flow, is there and we move naturally into the white light.

Chakra Meditation

In my workshops and apprentice groups, we do a chakra meditation that I share with you below. Allow yourself enough time to do it, and a quiet, comfortable space. It is best to do it barefoot and sitting with your feet connected to the earth, or it can be done lying down. Take your time to travel slowly through each chakra, there is no need to rush. And be aware that if you have a problem visualising one or more of the colours, this can indicate an imbalance or weakness in that area.

We begin with visualising our feet, deep in the brown earth. We then visualise the brown of the feet chakra spiralling up from Mother Earth, through both of our legs and filling that space. As the brown moves up over the knees, it gradually becomes the colour red of the base chakra.

We see the red at the base of our spine and feel it flowing all around our base area, connecting us with our tribe. Then we visualise the red spiralling upwards into the orange of our womb, the place of a woman's power. All of the time, we observe the brown and the red flowing upwards into the orange. Gradually, we see the orange moving upwards to become the yellow of the solar plexus, the place of our emotions, gut feelings and animal instincts. We see, feel or sense the yellow colour which, then, moves up into the green of the heart chakra. The heart is where we hold people and things that we love. We see the green flow and spiral round the heart before it moves up to the thymus chakra, the high heart, the place of unconditional love. We observe which colour comes to us in the thymus area, whether it is pink, jade or turquoise.

The colour of the thymus continues upwards until it becomes the blue of the throat chakra, allowing us to speak and stand in our truth. We feel that blue flowing around our throat and jaw, moving up over the mouth and the back of our neck. Then we continue to feel the colours growing and merging, moving upwards, until the blue moves up into the indigo, the bluish-purple colour of our third eye. Our third eye is our eye of perception, allowing us to see beyond and within.

We are aware of the brown flowing continuously from our feet, spiralling through red, orange, yellow, green, the colour of the thymus, blue and indigo, moving upwards into the purple of the head chakra, the place of communication. The colour purple in this place opens our intuition and our superconscious. Gradually, the purple flows upwards into the tenth chakra, the white light above our heads, the place of communion where no words are necessary.

Then, gently, we can feel ourselves moving down with the white light, through all the colours of the chakras, back down to the brown of the feet chakra and of the earth.

When we stand in this position, connecting the white light of communion to the brown colour of the earth, we are connected betwixt and between. We are between the heavens and our great earth mother and holding that space.

As we allow the energies to flow through us from the earth to the heavens and from the heavens to the earth, we can become a standing wave, holding the space as those energies flow through us, not just for the healing of our own chakras, but for the earth herself. When we become a standing wave, we clear, beautify and balance our own chakras. At the same time, we allow the presence and energies of the multiverses to flow down through us and we keep a balance, stabilising the earth as she grows through her changes.

Slowly, we become aware of our breathing and aware of our feet grounded in the earth. We become aware of our breath and gently open our eyes.

I have recorded the meditation above with my own voice, accompanied by my drumming, to guide you. You can journey with it by visiting: https://www.celticsouljourneys.com/seabhean-journeys/#chakra

The Power Body

An important teaching, revealed to me on my journeying, is the power body. It is a teaching unique to me and is a vital tool for anyone following the Way of the Seabhean, to protect themselves on a daily basis and, especially, while doing the work.

The power body is a body of energy that we build up around us to hold our space and protect ourselves from energies surrounding us. It stops us picking up unwanted energies and prevents them from affecting us. It reflects back whatever energies are being projected towards us.

The power body is connected to the base chakra and the third eye. There is a simple exercise we can do every day to build it up as a protection around us.

When you wake in the morning, relax and breathe. Make sure that you are at home within yourself and that all the parts of you are back from sleep.

First, you make your right hand into a fist and push it into the base of your spine, so that you can physically feel that space. Then you pull up the muscles of your pelvic floor and rectum. Pull the cheeks of your buttocks together and begin to feel that energy building up. You draw that energy up from your base chakra, through your backbone. It should feel like a warmth moving up your backbone.

As you feel that, you continue to push your fist in as you pull the energy up, through your neck, over your head and direct it out through your third eye and all around your body. From your third eye, you see, feel and sense that power body building up around you to a depth of two or three inches. The power body is the shape of an egg with the rounded part beneath your feet and the pointed part above your head.

You place your other hand just over your solar plexus, three to four inches away from your body, so that you can almost feel your power body. Push slightly on it. Feel and hold that. Know that it is there.

Three or four inches is deep enough for the power body. If it is too extended, you could push your energy onto other people; if it is too tight, you could shrink yourself. You need to own your space. This is your own space in which you are meant to reside. You continue to build up the power body, drawing it up from the base, up your backbone, up your neck, over your head, out of your third eye and around your body. This is something I strongly suggest that you do every morning before you get out of bed. It is very powerful.

To begin with, you need to become aware of your power body three, four or five times a day. Feel it there when you go to the bathroom or have a cup of tea. Each time, you can say to yourself, "I feel it, it is there".

Every morning, you build that up. After about six weeks you find that, as soon as you click in, it is there. You could be talking to somebody in a queue, and it is there, it is holding you.

Wherever you go, you have that body around you and, instinctively, other people can feel it. Those with clear, inner vision, can see it, but less conscious people can feel it instinctively and will tend to leave you alone. When your power body is in place, any energies that are projected towards you can be reflected back without you having to engage with them. It is interesting to note where you do engage, because it indicates that you are holding on to something.

We deserve to protect ourselves, to stand in our power and be who we are meant to be. That is something we can practice. As women we need to claim and hold this space that is ours. Instinctively, some women do not want to take up space. We should not allow anyone else to take our space.

Some people like to extend their power body. That is ego. We do not need to do that. Some have a constricted power body; they pull it in too tightly. If we are in a group where we feel unsafe, we can extend it a little and, if somebody comes too close, we can put our hand up, palm outwards. Stop. Most indigenous people across the world use that gesture. That way, we hold our space. It is rare for people to break through that.

Occasionally we get somebody who is so much in their own purpose that they break right into our space and that can be a real shock. When we are in our power body, we find that people, instinctively, pick that up and step back. They give us the space that is ours by right of being a human sharing this sacred planet. After a while, we get used to holding that space for ourselves.

THE UPPER WORLD

In my tradition we have three realms: Lower World, Middle World and Upper World. We know that the lower realm is our roots that hold and ground us.

The Middle World is the trunk of the tree, our place of being. We have looked at how we operate in this reality and the many tools that are available to us.

Then we have the Upper World, the branches of the tree that grow from, and above, the trunk. This is our place of spirit. It is the place of our intuition, our superconscious. This is the realm where we connect to our spirit guides and helpers and to the angelics. It is our connection with source. Just as the Lower World is the place of shadow, the Upper World is the place of pure light.

I always begin in the Lower World when I work shamanically because I believe that it is essential for us to be grounded before we begin. If we do not have strong and proper roots, we will not be able to balance the Middle and Upper Worlds. In my classes, I always leave the Upper World to last, because we need to be interwoven and integrated into our present reality before we go into the Upper World.

Many people want to go straight into the Upper World and connect with spirit, without having their roots to keep them grounded. Like a tree that is heavy with fruit but has no roots, they can become top-heavy. People can get tired or suffer from chronic fatigue, because they work a lot with spirit and have no roots to ground them. Over the years, I have met people who go straight up into the branches of the tree and get out of their bodies. They are in the Upper World but cannot pay their mortgage, do not like driving, or they shout and scream at their kids. They do not have the balance.

Often, we forget that we are spirit incarnate. We do not have to raise ourselves up to be in touch with spirit because we are the essence and presence of spirit in a physical form. Human beings are beings in a human form, so spirit is not something outside of ourselves. People often try to step out of where they are and out of their bodies to connect with the essence of spirit. But we do not have to leave our bodies, or go outside of ourselves, to find spirit. All we have to do is relax into that quiet space within us that is pure being. It is in that space, between the breath, that we connect into the realm of spirit.

This is just one of many lives through which the soul moves. The soul draws the energy needed to attract the teachings that we need in this lifetime and that attracting energy is the spirit energy. When we see a child who is full of energy, we say that she is spirited. It is that spirit energy within us that attracts what we need in this life.

We are here to live in the entirety of who we are. Therefore, we need to be grounded, so that our roots hold us as we open up. The stronger our roots, the more we have the ability to open up and flower into the essence. Just by being and living consciously, in truth and kindness, we can be everything that we were meant to be and we can affect the whole.

We all have a guide, a spirit helper that walks with us in life (what the Catholic Church calls our guardian angel). They are not there to tell us what to do; they are there to hold our hand. They do not walk in front or behind, but beside us. Whether we are aware of it, whether we fight it or not, they are with us constantly. We have other guides who can come in and walk with us too.

Just as we journey down to the Lower World, we journey upwards to the Upper World. As with our Lower and Middle World journeys, we begin by going to our place of safety and sitting beside our tree or stone. Our totem here is a spirit guide or spirit helper.

If you look at a diagram of the Tree of Life, you can see that the lower branches come down and almost touch the ground. The top roots come round and almost come back up, because there is a connection between the ancestors and our spirit guides.

When we connect with spirit guides and/or angelics, it is important to realise that they have no idea of time, or of our physical needs.

They are not going to help us find money, or the man or woman of our dreams. They do not have that concept. In England, I knew a medium in her sixties. When she was in her twenties, spirit told her that she would meet her soul mate. After about three years, she met a man. They married and had three children. Then, he had an affair and they separated. She felt let down, not just by him but, by spirit. About eight years before I met her, she met a wonderful man. It was one of those moments when their eyes met and they knew that it was right. They really merged together. She asked spirit, "Why did it take so long?"

Spirit replied, "We told you that you were going to meet your soul mate. What's your problem?"

Spirit can help us, but we have to do the work. They do not have a concept of time and will not give us the lottery numbers. They see things in a very different way.

Every one of us is on a path and we see other people on theirs. Sometimes they fall, scramble or become defeated; they help, or are helped by, others on the path. We cannot judge any of that.

We have the essence of spirit within us and our personal, spirit helpers walk beside us to hold our hand. But there are times when they can help us and times when they cannot get in, because we are in a place of darkness and despair. Spirit helpers and angelics are pure light and that is why they use intermediaries.

We live in the shadow, between darkness and light and can move into light and into darkness. Spirit is pure light. Wherever there is light, there is no darkness, only shadow. If we open ourselves to the presence of that light and allow it to come through us, that can help others.

Angelic forms often take a human body. Somebody will be moved to do or say the perfect thing at the time without knowing why. In that way, they can work through us. When there is a catastrophe, there is often a massive spirit energy holding that space. Angelics are often present when somebody is passing over. Family members can also be there for that person. They come in those times to hold that space.

When people tell me that spirit, or the masters, told them what they have to do, I just smile and go on my way. I believe that spirit would never say what you must do. In my thirties, I had a very deep experience and realised that spirit can advise us and assist with our choices, but we are here to be human beings, taking responsibility and making those choices for ourselves.

We are spirit in matter and have to take responsibility for our own choices. Spirit is there to assist us. They cannot do it for us. Once, they said to me, "Your choice is our command. If you choose to do that, we will work with you to assist you, but it is your choice."

If our spirit guides and helpers told us what to do, we would lose our power as human beings. The whole essence of the shamanic work is to help people to become empowered and conscious within themselves, not disempowered or less conscious.

We cannot sit at home and think that spirit is going to bring us everything we need. When we ask them for help, they bring energy which we have to direct into what we need. This life is all about taking responsibility, realising that we are the creatrixes and it is essential that we create. In the 1980s, spirit said to me, "You have to take responsibility. You are grown up now. You are not children of god anymore; you are adults of god." We have to take that role, step into that space betwixt and between, connected, in the Middle World, between the ancestors in the Lower World and the angelics and spirit guides in the Upper World.

We are spirit in matter, animal-human-spirit, a combination of ancestors, human and spirit in one. That is why we connect to our spirit guides who also help us to cultivate our intuition and superconscious.

Spirit can open our awareness to a greater view. We can imagine being in the woods and unable to see much, but if we climb a tree to the top, we have a much wider vista. From there, we can see a way out and see all that was invisible to us when we were down in the woods. Spirit gives us a better understanding of where we are or what is happening around us.

Both instinct and intellect are personal. In the Upper World, when we move into the superconscious, the higher self, it takes us out from the personal into the impersonal. Spirit helps us to move into that place and to shift our consciousness from self to non-self. We see from a wider angle. Once we understand things from that greater viewpoint, we begin to see that everything is part of the big picture of life itself.

Through the shamanic work, we can move out from the dependency of our instinctive reactions and become more human and independent, waking up and taking responsibility for our own lives. Then, when we go into the space of spirit we realise that we are an integral part of the whole and are interdependent. Being part of that greater reality does not diminish us, it strengthens and empowers us.

WOMEN'S MYSTERIES

MANY TRADITIONS HAVE WOMEN'S MYSTERIES. WE CALL them mysteries because they are held and hidden in the darkness.

My understanding of women's mysteries comes from within my bones, from my DNA. It comes from accessing ancestral memory of my foremothers who always honoured these times in their lives and made them sacred. It goes way back and I believe it is indigenous to us. Traditionally, women have been the holders of the sacred. We carry the chalice. It is natural to us to do that. This has always been recognised.

In many cultures and religions today, darkness equates to the devil and to things that are negative or bad. Yet, as women, we know that seeds grow in darkness. Darkness is our time of rest and respite, our time of filling ourselves again, so we are ready. In both hemispheres of the world, the day is filled with light and darkness in equal proportions during the year.

Light and darkness are a reflection of each other. Pure light is the absence of darkness and pure, black darkness is the absence of light. In between is a whole stream of colour. All colours together make white. When there is no colour at all, we have black. Both are important.

We tend to focus upon the light because, like every living thing on earth, we stretch and grow towards light. Yet, if we look at a tree, the roots go down into the darkness of the earth, as much as the shoots grow towards the light. As women, we recognise instinctively that we need to reclaim our darkness.

Our darkness is not bad or evil. In the darkness of our wombs, there is power that can be used to create and to formulate our plans, ideas and dreams. The womb is our place of sacredness in which they germinate.

Awakening Our Magic Through Our Blood

Traditionally, a woman's blood was used in magic. It was considered sacred and potent. In prehistoric times, it was used in ceremonies and to call upon the Great Mother. Ancient peoples used it and believed that, if they made love to a woman when she was bleeding, they could draw upon her power.

Most indigenous cultures of the world have celebrated when a young girl started her first blood. If she bled, it meant that, in time, she could bear children so the tribe would continue. It also moved the young girl from being with children to being with women. She began to take on more women's work. In some tribes they tied her hair in plaits, painted her face, or gave her tattoos to mark the transition. At first blood, the young girl is growing from a child into a young woman. She begins to carry responsibility. It was a time of great festivity.

Throughout the ages, a woman's blood has always been seen as potent. When she bleeds, that is potency and power, the time when she can dream. If they could, most women would look for time to themselves during their bleeding time. It is a time of gathering within ourselves. There is deep magic in that. That is what we see as the women's mysteries.

A mystery is something that we do not fully understand. In religion, they talk about the great mysteries, but I am talking about the mystery that each woman carries within her. We have not tapped into all that we are as women. To access that, we need to establish a connection into our wombs. We need to take advantage of our bleeding and learn how to work, dream, attract and sing with it and how to roar with it. When we harness that mysterious power, we ourselves are the mystery. It is no longer confined to our wombs, but infuses our whole being. We can begin to work with that in ways that are in harmony with our nature.

In today's world, young girls are not brought up to understand their bleeding time as a time of magic and dreaming. They resist it, fight it and do not want it. Some young girls take pills so they do not bleed at all and that affects their bodies. If they actually go with the blood and allow it to flow, see it flowing in their mind's eye, feel themselves letting go, then the blood will take all the toxins out of their bodies. It is a powerful thing to go with that rich, dark power that is flowing through us and to give it back to the earth, to the Great Mother. This is a creative force. The egg that is being carried by that blood had the potential to become a baby. How creative the energy of that blood is. We need to give that back to the earth.

Traditionally in Ireland, the woman's blood was given to the land. Even in my mother's time, they did not have tampons or sanitary towels. They picked moss and put it between two pieces of white cotton. When that was soaked, they put the moss into the earth. There was powerful symbolism in returning the blood of the womb to the earth. Men cannot bleed in that way, so some of them get their power through bloodshed.

This gathering of the blood and gifting it back to the earth is a sacred thing. It is good for young girls to actually sit on the earth when they menstruate and to make a little hole in the earth with their fingers and allow the blood to flow into it. That way, they gift it to the Mother, rather than flushing it down the toilet. Giving it back to the earth is part of our magic.

The basis of women's mysteries is getting in touch with the raw power of that blood and using it to bring energies, creativity and passion into our lives. We have seen how we can manifest our dreams, using the creativity of the womb to create the reality that we wish to attract for ourselves and for the planet.

As women we have a whole realm within us. Even if we no longer have a womb, this realm is available to us. For hundreds of years women have been disempowered, but now we are in a place where we can reclaim our power, grace and passion. By opening to the magic of our blood, we can stand fully in the presence of ourselves as women.

How often do we recognise that we have a right to pleasure? Pleasure is an ancient ritual. We can allow ourselves to move into the flow of our own passion, whether that is sexual passion, passion for life, passion for art, or passion to move our bodies through dance. Allowing that passion to flow is the essence of life. Being passionate shows that we are alive. We hold that passion in our wombs. That is true even if we no longer bleed.

As women, we have many faces. We can shapeshift into mothers, daughters, lovers, friends, healers and nurturers. It is important that we do not lose ourselves in any one of these roles, seeing ourselves only as a mother, lover or nurturer. These are just some of the many facets that make up the whole person that we have the potential to be. We also carry within us the goddess archetypes that we encountered when we worked with the Wheel. Connecting with those archetypes helps us to become whole.

Carrying the Chalice of Life and Creativity

The chalice is symbolic of the woman's womb. In the Arthurian legend of the Holy Grail, Percival met the Fisher King. A woman passed by holding a chalice which was running over with red wine or blood. "This cup that bleeds," the Fisher King said, "what is it for?" Percival could not answer him.

Our womb is our chalice. It is the cup that bleeds. What is it for? It gives life to humanity. This is our potency and strength. We need to be aware of the life force that we carry in our womb, how we can use that and, also, how we can abuse that.

We have the ability to physically give birth and to physically destroy. Because we can give life, we can also bring death. We are the birth mother and the death crone. Our words can heal or wound. Our hands can hold or kill. How often have we seen something we said lift or hold another? And how often have we seen our words hurt or harm another?

There is an old Irish saying that a woman who is very angry can make a vegetable go rotten, make meat go off, or turn butter rancid. There are many stories about that. They never talk about men doing that, but women can. Imagine what we could do if we used that potentially destructive ability in a way that was healthy, productive and life-giving? Whatever we do must be done with harm to none, otherwise it will come back to us. It is really powerful to work with our wombs and our blood and to cultivate and harness that energy in a positive way.

Opening to the Ability to be the Containers

In my tradition, I also see the chalice as the woman's ability to hold space for others. As we grow in consciousness and follow the Way of the Seabhean, we can embrace our Lower, Upper and Middle Worlds and blend our understanding of that with the women's mysteries. We can marry the two together and integrate them into our lives.

When our shamanic path is enhanced by the energies of our womb and of our blood, we can embody that way of being, so that we become the containers. As well as drinking from our own chalice, we can allow others to drink from it. We open to the ability to hold that space for others. That is the role of the Seabhean, of the priestess.

Our Irish stories tell us that many of the goddesses had priestesses. We have already mentioned the priestesses of Medb, one of whom lay with a chieftain at Tara on Bealtaine eve. It is said that Tlachtga also had priestesses. The goddess Brigit had priestesses who kept her fire alight. Later, it is likely that St Brigid's nuns held a priestessing role, before reforms in the Christian Church in Ireland excluded women and monks in favour of ordained male priests.

What does it mean, to priestess? For me, it means moving into the divine, while being fully present in our feminine and speaking through our hearts while holding the chalice. Each one of us is a chalice and within that we hold deep knowing, deep power and creativity. When we priestess, we hold that chalice for others to drink from so that they can be replenished by it and go forth and grow in the way that is meant for them. Our chalice never empties. It should fill us first, before we offer it to others, so that they can partake of it.

As Women We are Sisters

Part of the women's mysteries is awakening to the recognition that, as women, we are sisters. We have a sense of sisterhood of which some women are not aware. Women bleed together. At one point or another, we all find ourselves bleeding in unison with the women around us.

Every woman I meet, for me, is a potential sister. I recognise that we can share together and move beyond the boundaries of separation into the presence of being. Throughout humanity's time, as we know it, women have always come together (and still do in many indigenous cultures), to grow food, grind it, cook, weave, gather water, to help one another in bearing children, or in burying loved ones. Every woman is capable of participating in a community. It is in our nature.

When women come together magic happens. I proved that in London when I started a coffee morning with local women who were not overtly spiritual. One came and then more, as they told each other about it. I said nothing about spirituality or meditation. Each woman had time to talk and to share her experiences. It was not long before one of the women said to me, "Amantha we'd like to do meditation". So we did meditation. Then one of them asked about healing, so we started doing healing and sending light and love to all the people in need. Gradually, many of those women began to wake up spiritually.

I also did work with a few women who were involved in the Greenham Common women's peace camp. Those women had camped out at the Royal Air Force base, to protest against the storage of weapons of war and destruction there. They found that they were changing as they shared and lived together. Their spiritual energies started to evolve and flow. They went from being activists to being spiritual activists in a way.

In each of these groups, I witnessed women coming together and sharing and how that experience evoked their spirituality. I experienced, then and many times since, that when women come together and share with each other, something deeper happens. To me that is pure magic.

Our bodies carry our stories. We are our stories and we need to own them. When we come together as sisters, we tell our stories. Both the telling and the hearing of a woman's story is a powerful healing.

When women come together, we begin to remind each other, even unconsciously, of the magic that lies within us. As we learn to be together as sisters, we become whole. We find succour in each other. Together, we can find that deep space of loving, supporting and caring. This allows us to grow stronger, so that we can face whatever we are holding that needs to be faced in our outer and inner realms. As sisters, we can rebalance things, weaving the web through sound, through dreaming and weaving. Together, we can weave and mend, enhancing the Great Weave more effectively than we ever could as individuals.

RITUALS AND RITES OF PASSAGE

Rɪтuals and rɪтes of passaɢe have тraдɪтɪonally been used as an expression of transitional periods in people's lives. Many of us have ached to honour these times and by recognising and expressing them, we heal ourselves and weave ourselves whole again. Women's rites of passage bring sacredness into our lives, allowing us full expression of ourselves in a sacred manner.

Rites of passage are important for recognising times in our lives that have meant something to us. Once we recognise and honour those pivotal points, they become a part of our nature, rather than something protruding and not aligned with the rest of ourselves.

There is a difference between ritual and ceremony. Both are sacred and are done differently. Ritual can be done on one's own, or with two or three people to observe, bear witness, or participate in it. A ceremony usually involves a community celebration.

Ritual helps to bring things into balance. It helps us to absorb, honour and recognise all that we are. We can release through ritual and completely own what we need to own. It is the symbolism and intention behind a ritual that gives it power.

Women have always come together in ritual and celebration. We can imagine women gathering again in circles of sacredness, healing and holding. Our DNA retains the memories of those circles and we can evoke them to find the natural way for the individual and the tribe to celebrate and honour the changing seasons within our lives.

Our soul yearns to acknowledge the changing phases in our lives. When we honour those transitional times and experiences in our lives, we come home to the soul, recognising our spiral journey as one of unfolding and beauty. Celebrating these passages allows us to grow and to recognise and integrate those experiences, so that they do not become an unheard note within the family weave, to be experienced again and again through generations, until acknowledged and honoured.

In modern Ireland we grew up with mostly Catholic rituals and rites of passage, but these retained elements of the older pagan traditions. The early Christian Church, under Pope Gregory, had a policy of tolerating local customs, rather than trying to eradicate them. As a result, many of those customs survived side-by-side with, or integrated into, the Christian ceremonies.

For example, in the Irish tradition of death and burial, we have the church funeral, but we also retain the Irish wake. Until quite recently, there was the custom of the three Marys – three women called Mary, who would cry and tear their hair out, leading the mourners by their keening. That ritual goes away back to pre-Christian times.

The keeners were always elder women. Traditionally, it was women who helped women to give birth. Women helped people to pass over. In Ireland, we have always been familiar with the role of women as holders of that space. All over the country, there are symbols of the Cailleach, the hag, the crone. The Sheela-na-gigs (*Síle na gcíoch* – Sheila of the breasts – ancient carved images of women displaying enlarged vulvas, often found at the entrance to churches), which are symbols of the divine feminine, remind us that we are born of the womb and return to the tomb. These symbols are all around our land and we breathe them in without even knowing it.

Newgrange and Loughcrew were places of ritual and we can only surmise what rituals they held there. However, we know that before the coming of the patriarchal church, the society was matrifocal and it is possible that, before that, it was matriarchal. Women's rituals lie in the recesses of our memories despite attempts, over centuries, to eradicate them.

My granny had some rituals that were particular to her and some that were common at that time, rituals around cleaning the house, lighting the fire and saying grace before meals. Those kind of rituals are rarer now. In recent years there has been a movement away from church ceremonies, with people celebrating their life passages in ways that feel more authentic to them.

Going into ritual or ceremony is taking something special and making it sacred. Making things sacred is something that comes naturally to most women. Our bodies know how to do this.

Through moving into the sacred place of ritual, we give ourselves up to the experience. I might plan the ritual and say, "I'm going to do this here and I want you to say this and bring that in there", but the most important part of that ritual is that, when we step into it, we let go of all the pieces of it and allow it to move through us. Although we might plan to say certain words, something more might come through us and we need to allow that to happen. We need to let the ritual take us over. When that happens it becomes much deeper, as if the pulse of the earth moves through us, deep and ancient. This ritual has been done a hundred thousand times by other women before us. When we give ourselves into that ritual, we draw from the experience of all those women and it changes things for women. I have seen it again and again.

We can have rites of passage for anything that shifted or changed us. It could be for a relationship that we did not recognise for what it was and, when we did, it was really painful. Maybe that person had been lying to us and we say, "Why did it take me so long to see this?" Instead of blaming ourselves for it, let us honour the process that we have been through. Let us honour the pain and that our heart was innocent enough to be naïve about it. Let us honour the fact that we had to let go of that naïveté, which was a beautiful, childlike thing within us. We can do a ritual around that, to gather ourselves back and release that energy, so that we no longer attract people of that ilk back into our lives. When we have a ceremony, we grasp it, own it and transition accordingly. Our lives will never shift if we do not.

There is no point in hoping that everything is going to change, that a new job and a new lover will come in and that we can still be the same person. We have to change and, then, everything around us will change. That is the real power of ritual and of rites of passage.

If we do a ritual around some experience that was very painful or difficult, we instruct our instinctive bodies to move on and to let go of that experience. We do it by gifting ourselves a deep experience of that transition. When we move into the sacred, we also move into a form of psychodrama. That goes deep down into our bones and our psyche. Words are not enough to do that. A ritual or a ceremony is something that we experience on a profound level.

In a ritual or ceremony, there is a beginning, a centre, a climax and a conclusion, where we come down out of it. Traditionally, one always fasted beforehand and broke one's fast afterwards with eating and drinking. People still do that today in many ceremonies like weddings and naming ceremonies. It is usual to eat, drink and make merry afterwards. Even when people pass over, in Ireland, we have a wake where people eat and drink.

Something as simple as cooking can be a ritual. There is a sacredness in the way that some people peel potatoes and cut carrots. They can find their own special space while they cook, so that they can focus on the intention of the meal that they are preparing for themselves and others. Intention is central to ritual.

Ceremonies are performed with communities. People come together for naming ceremonies, union ceremonies and celebrations of life (for those who have passed on). Many of these were later taken by different churches and made into sacraments. We are familiar with baptisms, weddings and funerals as community church ceremonies, but these rites of passage existed long before that.

The main rites of passage that we celebrate are: birth; first naming; first blood (for a girl); puberty (for a boy); first love; union; giving birth; grief; separation; mastectomy/hysterectomy; change of life; last blood; croning; facing our death; celebration of life.

As part of my work, I facilitate rites of passage. It is one of my passions. A guided meditation associated with this chapter, the Grandmothers' Meditation, has been recorded in my voice and you can listen to it on: https://www.celticsouljourneys.com/seabhean-journeys/#grandmother

1 Birth

Birth is a rite of passage. It is our first breath in life. We grew in our mother's womb and that was our universe. Then most of us went through the journey of birth, travelling through the birth canal. It is said to be the hardest journey ever and that it prepares us for life. Children born by caesarean section do not have that experience. Because they are born without the pressure of having to push and get out, sometimes they have difficulty in closing, finishing or staying with things.

Traditionally, women were with women for birth. In different parts of the world, women gave birth in various positions: standing up, hanging on to a tree, in water, in the sea, or using birthing chairs or stools. The practice of lying down on a table or bed to give birth is relatively new.

In Ireland, people called upon Brigit as the midwife when they assisted with births. I was never with Granny in her role as midwife, but whenever she met a newborn for the first time, she put a sixpence into the palm of their hand, closed the fingers over it and then kissed the pulse on the inside of their wrist. *"Ádh mór, a chroí,"* (Good luck, my love), she would say, "may you never know hunger or thirst." That was a tradition that was very important to Granny. People would put that sixpence under a statue of the Child of Prague and keep it for the child.

2 Naming

A naming ceremony is called a baptism in the Christian Church. It is normally a ceremony rather than a ritual, because it is a clan celebration. Naming can happen at any age but is usually for children up to the age of four or five, depending on the people and the part of the world in which they live.

Names have power and vibration. In our tradition, children were given names of their ancestors. My birth name, Ellen Mary, was after Granny, my mother's mother, the one who taught me. My brother was called after my dad's father. So we continue to hold the energy of that vibration coming down through the ancestors. That pattern of naming has changed in Ireland since the advent of television in the 1970s.

As we have seen, in some tribes where the child is treated as if they are the ancestor after whom they were named, they can sometimes access that ancestor's memories within their DNA. There is power in the names we use.

When we do a naming ceremony, I usually ask the family to find out what the name means and, knowing that, whether they still want to call the child by that name. They can also find a second name. The family is involved in the ceremony. I ask the grandparents to offer their blessings for the child. We normally have a bowl of small crystals and each of the baby's little cousins chooses one for the baby and receives one "from" it. Each child comes up with a ribbon and ties it on to a little sapling, as their gift to the newborn baby. It is lovely when they come up and say, "I promise to play with you" or "I'm not going to let anybody beat you up at school". They are embracing the child as part of their family and getting to know them from that early age. It is powerful.

3 First Blood

Through accessing my ancestral memories, I have understood that first blood was a time of great celebration in Ireland. When a girl began bleeding, it meant that the tribe would continue. That is the absolute opposite of what happens today, where menstruation is often considered a nuisance or a "curse". Nowadays, first blood can be quite traumatic for the child. It was a time when the girl left playing with other children and started to assist her mother and aunts. Her hair might be braided or her ears pierced. How many young girls now get their ears pierced at that time? Can you imagine having a celebration because you had your first bleeding?

In 2009, when my eldest granddaughter was eleven, she rang me up to ask, "Would you do a ceremony for me?" She came over to Ireland with her younger sister and her mother, my daughter. Another of my daughters, her aunt, was also there. I gathered about seven women, half of whom were crones, and we did a ceremony. Her younger sister sat in the corner and drummed throughout, so she was an integral part of it. My daughters brought my granddaughter in, standing one on either side of her.

I stood outside the circle with my staff and said, "Who cometh here?" One of my daughters introduced my granddaughter, stating her matrilineal line. "And why is she here?"

My other daughter answered, "She is here to be accepted into the circle of women. She has had her first blood." I moved my staff to one side and my granddaughter stepped into the circle and each of the women blessed her. We had a beautiful ceremony with her in the centre of the circle and the elder women around her. My grand-daughter really felt fed by it and said that it supported and helped her afterwards. It was lovely that she asked me.

Now, all around the world, women are doing celebrations of first blood. They have what they call red tent ceremonies with young girls for their bleeding ceremony. The women get a tent, dye it red and get red cushions and rugs and throw them on the ground. They bring the girls into this redness, which is symbolic of the womb. For women, there is nothing more nourishing than being held in a womb energy. That is where we grew from and grew through. It is a very sustaining energy.

It is important to honour the bleeding time and to give our blood back to the earth. How many girls go through terrible pains because they are pulling those muscles up to hold a tampon when the blood is pushing to come out? They do not want their blood. They consider it dirty. Imagine wanting and honouring that. Traditionally bleeding was always a rite of passage where the girl moved into the clan of the women.

4 Boys' Rite of Passage

When a boy reaches puberty, it is his time for a rite of passage. In Ireland, traditionally, that was the time when he first went out with the men to cut turf. Any man will tell you that cutting turf is the hardest job. It was a back breaking experience for the young boy, but he could not complain. At the end of the day, the men took that boy out and bought him a drink, his first pint of Guinness, or whatever it was. Then, he was no longer a boy, he was a man. That was his rite of passage. We do not have that anymore, but we are in a culture where those rites of passage have been enacted throughout time. Many young boys have no way of going through that rite of passage, so they create their own rites, driving cars at night on the back roads, trying to do something to bring themselves through that transition.

5 First Love

For many, the next major rite of passage is first love, the first time their passion is awoken on that deep, deep level. Love is celebrated in many of our Irish stories, The *Pursuit of Diarmuid and Gráinne, Deirdre of the Sorrows, Oisín in Tír-na-nÓg* and, of course, *The Story of Bran.* We also have a tradition of beautiful love songs including *Eleanor a Rún* (Eleanor my secret love), *Ceann Dubh Dílis* (dark-haired faithful one) and She Moved through the Fair. There is a rich tradition of love poems in Irish, but sadly, my dyslexia has prevented me from reading or mastering the language to enjoy them.

6 Handfasting

In my tradition we had a handfasting ceremony rather than marriage. Handfasting is a ceremony of union, where two people come together. It is where the phrase "tying the knot" comes from, because traditionally, the couple's hands were joined together and ribbons were wound around them. Marriage, as we know it, came in quite late with the Christian Church.

I often do handfasting ceremonies with couples. Handfasting is the coming together of two tribes. The woman comes in with her tribe behind her and the man comes in with his. I have a semicircle of turf on the ground. Two people stand with her, often her mother and father, or maybe her mother and aunt. The man also stands with two people and I ask who they are. They say who they are. I ask, "Why are you here?" Then, the couple take each other's hand and step inside the semicircle. Everybody else stays outside. With each ribbon they have to say something. I ask if they want to be joined in union and they say, "We do". So the bond is made and then the ribbons are tied. I usually make a joke, "Tie it good and tight so they can't get away". Of course, it isn't that tight – they can slide their hands out.

From their union comes the union of the two tribes. Traditionally, the marriage brought peace between those two tribes.

In today's world people are not always aware of what it means to hold fast with another, to handfast with another, to commit to walking a path together. The journey does not end at that point with happily-ever-after. Their journey begins. They begin to learn how to work and operate together, how to dance together, sometimes with one leading, sometimes with the other. Some people have been brought up to be so independent that they find it hard to compromise. We can never compromise ourselves, but there are times when we need to learn how to bend, work, love and make decisions together. That all grows after we have chosen to be together.

7 Giving Birth

You go through a huge transition when you give birth to a child. That is a rite of passage.

On a number of occasions, I have been with women, including my two eldest daughters, for births. The midwife, or the nurse takes care of the birth itself and the baby, whereas I take care of the woman. I have her breathing and focusing on me and I may also have worked with her throughout the pregnancy. It works very well.

Nowadays, the word they use is 'doula'. The doula tradition is worldwide, not from any single culture. I had never heard the word until I was with my eldest daughter in America, when she was having her first baby. Now one can be trained to become a doula, which is a wonderful gift.

8 Separation

When we separate from somebody with whom we have been, it is a death for which we need to grieve. It needs to be recognised and honoured.

"Oh no, we split up ages ago…" This is something we hear more and more these days. Our souls choose the teachings we need in order to grow and our greatest growth often seems to come through our personal, intimate relationships. Yet we still need to deal with the pain, hurt and anger on many levels. This is where a separation ritual can be powerful in bringing closure to the relationship.

I create a sacred space where the couple comes together in ceremony to recognise, acknowledge and release the roles each took in the other's life. I hold the space for the couple, first to talk and then to release the dreams that they shared and worked on, mutually and for each other. They move on to thank each other for the lessons and gifts that they have brought to one another. I have found that sharing this rite of passage with one or (preferably) both partners of the relationship gives each the opportunity to recognise the cycle of birth, growth and death within the relationship. From this, many have found that they can grow and move on, conscious of what they no longer need to carry forward into future relationships. I offer this as a rite of passage that is sorely needed for heart healing.

Out of five couples with whom I did separation ceremonies, over a period of two years, two couples came back together. One woman had been working on herself through the Way of the Seabhean. Then, she and her partner came to me to do the separation ceremony. Because of what they shared, they decided to stay together, which I think is wonderful. Through the shamanic work, she had evolved and opened up and had not given him time to grow and evolve to meet her. She had changed dramatically and was not the woman he had fallen in love with, but he wanted to get to know her again. It was beautiful to see the change in them.

9 Surgery

We can honour major surgeries such as mastectomy and hysterectomy as rites of passage and it can be helpful for women to recognise them as such. The ritual can be done before or after the operation. A mastectomy ritual can honour the changes in her body and what has been lost. It can mark the transition, usually from cancer, into the wholeness of health after the operation, accepting and embracing the new shape of her body, seeing the scars as part of her story and the whole process as part of her soul journey. In that way, the mastectomy is not just about loss, it is also seen as part of her growth into the entirety of who she is.

A hysterectomy ritual honours what the woman has carried in her womb. There could be a little altar with things that she has created, whether that is her children, books or other works of art. If she is a therapist, it could be the names of people she has helped. Through that, she can see her life as a creative venture and she is now moving into a new form of creativity.

10 Grief on the Death of a Loved One

Grief is a rite of passage. When we lose somebody we love, that sorrow has to go somewhere. Granny used to say that you need to give yourself a year and a day to grieve. Traditionally, the community supported you in that. People came round with food or porter (beer), they talked about that person with you and allowed you to talk. Whether they were our mother, father, brother, sister, husband, wife, son, daughter, nephew or niece, we need to talk about that person. They were important in our lives and we must allow ourselves to grieve. That has to flow through us before we can move on. Often, nowadays, people move on really quickly, but they may not have given themselves time to grieve.

Traditionally, in Ireland, there were keeners at funerals. The word keen comes from the Irish word *caoin,* to mourn. Keeners were women who cried on behalf of the community. By letting themselves wail and cry aloud, they gave the mourners permission to release their grief. Sometimes, in my workshops, we have keening sessions. Some women need to keen for hours. We hold the pain of our mothers and grandmothers. When they were not able to express their grief, that pain went inside them. As an egg in our grandmother's womb, as an embryo, and then a foetus, in our mother's womb, we take on that grief. Growing up, we instinctively absorb grief around us. We watch the women around us, whether they are able to allow themselves to grieve or not, and we take that on too. Generations of grief is carried within us. It is powerful to let that grief come forth.

When we give ourselves permission to keen, we do that for all of the women who could not, or were not allowed to. We keen for all the women whose voices were stilled and made silent. Keening together we connect on a deep level of sisterhood and family.

11 A Woman's Change of Life – A Time of Self-Empowerment

We have a rite of passage for the woman's change of life (perimenopause). This time, for a woman, usually begins between the ages of forty-one and forty-eight and can go on until fifty-five. It is a time when her children are growing up and leaving home and she does not have to put all of her energy into the family anymore. Her bleeding is slowing down, she is not ovulating in the same way and, instead of being given for the tribe, that creative energy is there for her to gather for herself. It is her time of gathering her gifts to her. This rite of passage celebrates the woman coming into herself. It is a time of claiming all that she is. We were taught to give our gifts away for others, but now, we use those gifts for ourselves.

Often change of life can coincide with "empty nest syndrome". It is the time when a woman can look at what she can do for herself. What does she enjoy? How does she want to express herself? What does she want to do with her life? What did she dream about and are those dreams still relevant today? Now that she has more time and space for herself, she might like to write, dance, play an instrument, play bridge, or start travelling. It could be anything. This is a time of gathering what she wants for herself. She can begin to put together a bundle or bag, in which she can put things that mean something to her. In that way, she becomes empowered.

12 Last Blood

Traditionally, last blood and becoming a crone (hag, elder, Cailleach) were considered to be the same thing. Last blood has now become separate from croning. Many women finish their bleeding in their early fifties and are not ready to be a crone. Women live longer now.

When we finish bleeding, our bodies go through a transition. Our monthly cycle is finished and we begin to access more of our magic. We have moved through motherhood and have time and vitality to make choices about what we want to do.

One woman, who shared her wisdom with us, said, "In my twenties, I was always worried about what people thought of me. In my forties I didn't care about what people thought of me. Now that I am in my sixties, I realise that people never did think about me." That is the way it should be. If we want to wear purple hats with feathers, why not? This is our time.

We do not have to fit in anymore. Energetically we are calmer. Whatever we have chosen to work through should be completed. This is our time to play, have fun and be wild. We can practise wildness and eccentricity now so that, when we get to that age, we know how to do it. As souls we have contracts with other souls to play certain roles in each other's lives. Often, by last blood, those commitments are completed. We can allow ourselves to relax.

Instead of following our menstrual cycle (traditionally called our moon time), bleeding and ovulation, we now follow the phases of the moon itself. The full and new moon become important times of meditation, in place of our bleeding time. We can use the moon's energy and work with its rhythm. How can we use and direct that energy?

As part of the timing of last blood, we move into a new space and allow the space, where we were, to be there for others. That is happening to me. Other people are doing work that I did and are attracting in younger women. I think that is great. It would not be right or healthy for me to hold that space.

13 Croning

When we are ready, we have the crone ceremony. As a crone, we can look back to the phases of our life. In the Irish tradition, we are familiar with three aspects of the woman: maiden, mother and crone. There is also the wild, unpredictable, mad or crazy woman, the Sheela-na-gig. In our culture, the maiden is pure, untainted and innocent, the mother is the carer, the giver, the nurturer and the crone is the old woman who holds the space, tells the stories and takes care of the children. The wild, or crazy woman is a side that we seldom look at and that we might fear. If we reclaim that wild woman, it can help us to find a balance for ourselves.

As the crone we are maiden, mother and wild woman. We have the ability to be all. In our Irish tradition, the hag, the ancient one, holds the energy of the land. Everything returns to her. That connection with the Cailleach is symbolised across the landscape of Ireland and revered in Irish mythology. Loughcrew is called the Hill of the Hag. There is the Hag's Head at the Cliffs of Moher in Clare. From Carrowmore, in Sligo, one can see a mountain range in the shape of an old woman with a sagging belly – that is referred to as the Cailleach.

The crone was always cared for by the community. She was given respect as an elder. Nursing homes for the elderly are quite a recent phenomenon.

Having a croning ceremony is not traditional in Ireland because that transition happened naturally for most women. We do it as a ritual now because we have lost that natural turning in our lives. We no longer have the time, space or conscious recognition of the cycles in our life, so we celebrate a rite of passage to bring ourselves back to that recognition, which is innate in us.

14 Celebration of Life – Death

Death is a rite of passage for the person who has died, as well as for those who are left behind. Traditionally, in Ireland, when a person died, a wake was held in their house. The body was laid out in a room and people came to say goodbye, to speak about them and honour them. Food and drink were served and a party was held to celebrate their life. Members of the family kept an overnight vigil beside them, so that they were not left alone. At the funeral, keeners led the community in expressing grief.

For centuries, the church funeral fulfilled the role of celebrating the lives of the dead. Now, people can opt for less religious ceremonies that are more personally meaningful for them and their loved one. The ceremony involves the family and respects the beliefs of the participants. It is nearly always a community ceremony, giving neighbours and friends an opportunity to express their condolences to the relatives. Mourners have an opportunity to reflect on the life of their loved one and to give thanks for their life. They can bid their farewell and begin the process of grieving.

WEAVING
OUR WORLD

The world is a weave and each one of us is a thread on that Great Weave. Everything we do, experience and feel not only affects our personal weave but touches and colours the Great Weave that holds our blessed Mother Earth in space. As we change, grow, awaken and take responsibility, we activate a vibration that ripples out on the Great Weave where it can be drawn upon by all.

We are at a pivotal point in the evolution of humanity, where consciousness is breaking through across our sacred Mother Earth. It is coming as she dies and is reborn. We midwife that too, through our intentions and dreams, through every choice we make, every minute of every day, and through everything we buy. Every word we speak is part of that rebirth. This is a huge time of change.

We have come back on this earth because we need to awaken to our teachings and because we have work to do. Part of that work is to assist other souls with their growth, whether that is in a good or a difficult way for them, or for us. We are also here to take responsibility for this living earth. There has to be a balance in everything. If I do a reading for you, you do something for me in return. Either you pay, feed or gift me something. There has to be an exchange. What is our exchange with the earth?

All the points of the Wheel, the ancient calendar, were earth festivals. They were celebrations of gratitude, blessing the earth and offering back to her. Traditionally, everything was given back to the earth. Leftover food was given to the animals. The pigs ate the swill. There were no dumps and there was no plastic. Groceries and goods were wrapped up in newspaper or cardboard and string. The packaging was burnt for fuel and the ashes went back to the earth. Drinks came in glass bottles that were washed out and recycled. Springs and wells were kept clean because the people were drinking from them. There were regular blessings of the wells. People treated the earth with great respect because they knew that their lives depended on her being healthy and fruitful.

When my mother was dying, we brought her home to Kerry. I cared for her, cooking food that she could eat, until she could no longer eat, and bathing her in bed. After she died, I washed her body. I did that because I loved her. She was and is my mother. Can we care for the earth in the same way? Why not? We cannot forget that the earth is our mother. To me, there is nothing more important than that.

Sometimes we close ourselves away from her rather than embracing her. Every day is a gift. First thing every morning, I open the curtains, look out and celebrate whatever the day is. Can I see my mountains or are they in shadow? Is there snow on them? Some foggy days, I cannot see anything out there but that is a gift too. It is saying to me, "Okay, can you take some time for yourself today? Can you close down a little?" Mother Earth is there for us all of the time and we need to take care of Her.

For millennia, people lived their lives dependent on the elements and the forces of nature. In the technological age, people in developed countries are detached from the natural world. Our technologies and defences cannot always protect us from natural disasters like floods, hurricanes and earthquakes. We might not think we are dependent on the earth, but we are.

We are meant to be the creators and creatrixes of this living planet and of our lives. That is why we are here. Not only do we have the tools to assist the earth in her process of death and rebirth, we are the tools through which the new planet will come into existence. We are part of the great energetic weave of the earth. Each time we participate in our own weaving, we affect the whole. Every one of us is a drop in the ocean of humanity and we can change the ocean with one drop.

We are aware of the earth's process of rebirth. Things have to be broken up or broken into to allow change to emerge. We are part of that change. If we allow ourselves to go into that struggle and are held by it, we are not holding that space of consciousness. We need to hold that still space within the storm, even though it is going on around us and flooding into our world.

One way to enable the birth of the new is to dream this new earth awake. How do we want to see this new earth and all that live upon her? We can dream for the planet by being in the presence and nature of all that we are and holding that space in our intentions, thoughts, words and deeds. In a similar way to creating our reality, we can consciously attract what we dream for the planet. We clarify what we wish to attract into our lives and our world, with harm to none. Then, we hold that visualisation. It is important not to get distracted by daydreams, to focus that vital force of electromagnetic power that we need in order to attract.

It sounds simple, yet most people cannot take twenty conscious breaths before they forget. We are being filled all the time with distractions to pull us away from that focus. That is no mistake. Those who hold power look for ways to keep us disempowered. The more powerful we become, the more we seek change. People all over the world are focusing on that change. The more conscious we are of feeding into and participating in that, the more it changes.

We all share a dream of peace, of children being safe, of food and water for all to share. It is a good, strong dream and the dream of the earth herself. By dreaming this true, this is the legacy we can leave behind. Future generations will see innovative, ecologically enhancing technologies come forth that will help with the ozone layer and with atmospheric changes. If we dream this for a few minutes every day, we will find ourselves aligning energetically with the earth. The greatest assistance we can give to the earth and to humanity is to dream true. As well as having the dream that we are bringing into reality for ourselves, we also share the dream of the earth. We can share it with all those who are dreaming it and with the earth herself. Through our consciousness we can become part of the transformation that is happening right here and now. We are the ones. This is the time. It is our responsibility.

As we align ourselves with the earth and stand in our consciousness, dreaming her dream, each one of us becomes a standing wave. That is a powerful way to midwife the new earth. We mentioned the standing wave in the context of the chakras. When we do the chakra exercise, feeling, sensing and seeing the colours moving up through us from the brown of the earth, into the white light, our place of communion, the place of being at one, that brings us into alignment with ourselves. Sitting in that place of the white light, we bring the energy down again through and around our body, vibrating with our colours, down and through the earth below. When we do that we connect and receive energies coming through from the multiverse, like a radio antenna that picks up signals, and bring that down into the earth.* By allowing that energy to flow through us, we can aid the planet at her time of transformation.

As well as having a dream, working on it, focusing and directing it, we need to live it. Part of living the dream of the earth is living with integrity and making sure that everything we participate in has integrity. This comes down to ensuring that food we buy is grown sustainably and with harm to none. If we feed into a system that is corrupt, that is what we put into the reality that we are creating for our children. We need to be quite aware of what we are leaving for future generations. This is the first time in about five generations that our children are worse off than we are. We have left them quite a destructive place to live, on many levels. The integrity that we put into what we buy and how we live will affect all the generations to come. We need to be conscious, even if it means that we have less. If we buy less, we need to do that consciously.

Our purpose is to live life in consciousness, with truth, love, harmlessness and kindness to others. If we live in full consciousness, congruent with our nature as soul essence, and recognise every person and every living thing as part of that, then that is the greatest service we

* The Chakra and Standing Wave Meditation is also available at: https://www.celticsouljourneys.com/seabhean-journeys/#chakra

can give. That consciousness brings us into that place of interconnection and interdependency on everything in life, be it a tree or plant, an animal, or the person who walks by us on the street. We would never hurt another human being if we recognised the essence of their being and that they are a part of us – we are all interconnected.

To follow the Way of the Seabhean, we consciously change the world purely by our participation in it. Consciousness is awareness that we are part of something greater than ourselves and that what we do affects others. Every time we claim life for ourselves, claim our voice or our truth, that affects all within our Great Weave. When we speak and stand, we change the weave for everyone. We can do more, but that is the least we can do. Sometimes we get caught up in our own dramas and forget that we are part of this living earth and have a role to play on our blessed planet.

As we grow, we affect everything around us, every living thing, every creature, every plant and the air itself. Each conscious breath is a sound and a frequency, a vibratory note that flows out into our multiverse, where others can inhale it and draw from it. It changes every space we inhabit and gifts others the opportunity to change also. As living organisms on this planet, we are all interconnected. We share the same breath.

As each one of us works on our own weave, we help to bring consciousness, stability and balance into the Great Weave. The most important thing on the shamanic path is to keep the weave in balance.

All the lives we have lived and are living are coming together and impacting on us. Those lives are weaving around us right here and now and we need to draw those energies in. We may have been dreamers in one life, weavers in another and soulsingers in another. One way of bringing those energies into the now is by consciously allowing ourselves to dream, weave and soulsing. By doing so, we draw everything into this place, space and time.

Living in full consciousness means that we have integrated all of our lives. That allows us to be fully cognisant and to be in the moment. When we are fully cognisant, we can be what we were always meant to be – the creators and creatrixes of our lives and of the new earth. In this space, we can be extraordinary.

Let us remember, if we can, that each time we place our feet consciously on the earth, it is a gentle prayer to the earth. Let us not forget to dream our dreams, to hold our intention. Let us join together in the great affirmation from the Way of the Seabhean – *"Sea!"* ('Sha!' – Yes!)

'SEA!

GLOSSARY AND PRONUNCIATIONS

Key Terms

NB. The stressed syllable is underlined.

seabhean: ('<u>sha</u>-van') The Irish female shaman, healer and seer.

sea: ('sha') Strength or vigour. Similar to neart below. Also regard or esteem.

'sea!: ('sha') Short form of 'is ea' meaning it is or yes.

Tuath Dé: ('<u>thoo</u>-a-day') Tribe of god. An older form of Tuatha Dé Danann ('<u>thoo</u>-ha day <u>Don</u>-on') tribes of the Goddess Danu. An ancient pre-Celtic tribe that ruled Ireland for millennia and were said to possess magical powers.

Goddesses

Áine: ('<u>awn</u>-ye') Irish goddess associated with the summer solstice.

Boann: ('<u>bowe</u>-an') Tuath Dé goddess of water and fertility. She gives her name to the river Boyne. Associated with the spring equinox.

Brigit: ('<u>bridge</u>-it') Ancient Irish goddess of Kildare, and later, an early Christian saint. Associated with Imbolc.

The Cailleach: ('<u>coll</u>-yuk') The hag or crone. An ancient deity much revered in Ireland. Associated with the winter solstice.

Ériu: ('air-<u>oo</u>') Goddess representing Ireland in the form of a woman. One of the three princesses of the Tuath Dé: Ériu, Banba ('bon-ba') and Fódhla ('foal-a').

Macha: ('<u>mock</u>-a') A sovereignty goddess of ancient Ireland and the Tuath Dé. Various Machas appear in Irish mythology, so it may be a title rather than a name.

Medb: ('mayv') Ancient earth goddess and later Queen of Connacht.

Tailtiú: ('<u>thol</u>-too') A goddess of the Tuath Dé and foster mother of the sun god, Lugh. Associated with Lughnasa.

Tlachtga: ('<u>thlock</u>-th-ga') Ancient Irish deity and daughter of the magician Mog Ruith. Associated with Samhain.

Anu: ('<u>an</u>-oo') The mother goddess associated with the Paps of Anu in County Kerry. The Firbolgs called her Aná, the Tuath Dé called her Anu and the Celts changed her name to Danu (pronounced 'Dhon-oo').

Morrigan: From the Irish *Mór Ríoghain* meaning great or phantom queen. A figure from Irish mythology associated with battle and death.

Sionann: ('<u>shun</u>-un') Goddess of the River Shannon.

Festivals of the Wheel

Samhain: ('<u>sow</u>-in' – sow rhymes with cow). Hallowe'en. An ancient Irish festival and the beginning of the Pre-Celtic new year. The most important festival of the Wheel of the year.

Imbolc: ('im-bulk') Old Irish. Sometimes translated as 'in the belly' – meaning the time when the ewes are with lamb. Brigid's Day – February 1st. Ancient spring festival of the Goddess Brigit.

Bealtaine: ('be-owl-thin-e') Old Irish. Possibly meaning bright fire. It is the Irish word for the month of May, as well as the ancient festival celebrated on the eve of May 1st. It is an important turning of the ancient Irish calendar.

Lughnasa (often spelt **Lughnasadh**): ('loo-na-sa') Translates as the assembly of the sun god, Lugh ('loo'). Ancient Gaelic festival on the eve of August 1st.

People, Places and Words

ádh mór, a chroí: ('awe more a cree') Good luck, my (sweet)heart.

Áed Rúad: ('ay roo-a') Red-haired Hugh. The father of Macha in the Emain Macha story.

Ailill: ('al-ill') Queen Maeve's lover in the story of the *Táin*.

anam cara: ('on-um corr-a') Soul friend.

Airmid: ('arri-mid') Herbal healer of the Tuath Dé.

banshee: An Anglicisation of *bean sidhe* ('ban-shee') fairy woman or woman of the Tuath Dé who wails to alert people that someone has died.

barm-brack: Anglicisation of *Báirín Breac* ('baw-reen brack'), the speckled loaf. A fruit bread eaten at Samhain.

Beanfeis: ('<u>ban</u>-fesh') The sacred marriage. The ritual union of the chieftain and a priestess of Medb at Tara on Bealtaine eve.

Biddies: People who dress up in straw cone hats that cover their faces and necks. On Brigid's Eve, they go from door to door, singing and dancing in all the local houses.

Blocc and **Bluigne:** ('bluck' and '<u>blig</u>-na') Two standing stones at Tara.

bó: ('boe') Cow.

bodhrán: ('<u>bower</u>-aun') An Irish, tambourine-like drum.

bothán: ('<u>bu</u>-hawn') Cottage.

Bran: The hero of a very early Irish story in which he travels to Tír na nÓg.

brat: ('brotth') A cloak or shawl.

Brian Boru: ('<u>bri</u>-an <u>bur</u>-oo') Anglicisation of old Irish Brian Bóruma. A High King of Ireland in the 11th century.

Brú na Bóinne: ('<u>brew</u> na <u>boe</u>-in-e') The palace or mansion of the Boyne. A Neolithic site in the bend of the River Boyne, containing numerous megaliths including Newgrange, Knowth and Dowth.

Cailleach Béara: ('<u>coll</u>-yuk <u>bear</u>-a') The hag of the Béara peninsula in County Cork in the southwest of Ireland.

caoin: ('queen') To cry.

Carrowkeel: From the Irish, *Ceathrú Caol,* the narrow quarter. A megalithic complex in the Bricklieve Mountains in County Sligo.

Carrowmore: From the Irish *Ceathrú Mór,* the big quarter. An important megalithic cemetery in County Sligo.

Cathair Crobh Dearg: ('<u>cahir</u> <u>crow</u> <u>darg</u>') Translated as Red Claw's city and locally known as Red Claw's Enclosure or The City. An enclosure at the sacred mountains of the Paps in County Kerry.

Cill Dara: ('<u>keel</u>-da-ra') Church of the Oak. Anglicised as 'Kildare' – a county and town in Ireland.

clouties: Pieces of cloth placed on a hawthorn bush for good luck at Bealtaine.

Cnoc Áine: ('cun-<u>uk</u> <u>awn</u>-ye') Anglicised as 'Knockainy'. Áine's Hill in County Limerick.

Cruinniuc: ('<u>krinn</u>-yuk') Macha's husband in one of the stories of Macha.

Cúchulainn: ('<u>koo</u>-cul-in') The hound of Culainn. Great hero of Irish mythology. Having accidentally killed Culainn's hound, he had to make recompense by guarding Culainn's property. So he became known as Cúchulainn. He was previously called Setanta.

Cul: ('cull') The father of Bran.

currach: ('<u>curr</u>-ock') A small traditional Irish boat, made with a wooden frame over which animal hides or skins were stretched.

Dagda: ('<u>dog</u>-da') Father god of the Tuath Dé. Associated with fertility, manliness, magic, druidry and wisdom.

Derrynane: ('derry-<u>naane</u>') A townland in County Kerry.

Diarmuid and **Gráinne:** ('<u>dear</u>-mid' and '<u>graw</u>-in-ye') Lovers in Irish mythology who eloped although Gráinne was promised to Fionn McCool.

Eamain Macha: ('<u>ow</u>-en <u>mock</u>-a') Sometimes translated as Macha's Twins. A large circular hilltop enclosure, now called Navan Fort in County Armagh. Armagh is from *Árd Mhacha* meaning Macha's Height.

Elcmar and **Neachtain:** ('<u>knock</u>-thin') Two of Boann's consorts.

filí: ('fill-<u>ee</u>') Plural of *file* ('<u>fill</u>-e') Poet.

Fourknocks: A smaller passage tomb in Brú na Bóinne. The name Fourknocks possibly comes from the Irish *Fuar Cnoc* meaning cold hill.

Fiachra: ('<u>fee</u>-a-kra') Queen Maeve's son.

Firbolgs: (Anglicisation of *fir bolg*, 'fir bulg') The men with the sacks, also known as the dark-haired ones. A race of giants who ruled Ireland before the Tuath Dé.

Fionn McCool: ('<u>finn</u> muc-<u>cool</u>') Fionn MacCumhaill. A legendary Irish hero and head of a band of warriors called the *Fianna* ('<u>Fee</u>-ana')

grianstad an gheimhridh: ('<u>gree</u>-an-stod un <u>gee</u>-rig') The winter solstice – literal translation 'winter sun-stop'.

handfasting: An ancient Irish marriage-like ceremony where the couple's hands are symbolically tied together.

immram: An Anglicisation of the Irish word *iomramh* meaning 'a mystical journey', usually to Tír na nÓg. It is a journey from which nobody can return the same. Plural immrama.

Kilgobnait: ('kill-gub-nit') The church of Saint Gobnait. Anglicised as 'Kilgobnet'. A townland in County Kerry.

Knocknarea: ('knock-na-ray') Translated as 'the hill of the moon'. A hill in County Sligo where Queen Maeve is said to be buried.

Knowth and **Dowth:** Two other passage tombs from the Neolithic period, in Brú na Bóinne.

Loughcrew: Passage tombs and a megalithic cemetery in County Meath.

Lugh: ('loo') The sun god, who was half Tuath Dé and half Fomorian.

Manannán Mac Lir: ('man-an-awn mac lir') The god of the sea who is said to be Boann's consort. The Isle of Man is called after him.

matrifocal tradition: A tradition where men, as well as women, have roles in honouring the divine feminine.

Midhe: ('me') Middle or centre. Irish name for County Meath.

Mog Ruith: ('mog rih') Mog of the Wheel. The Kerry magician who made the Wheel of the Sun and used it to time travel. The father of Tlachtga.

neart: ('nyarth') Strength or life force.

Nemods: ('knee-mods') The people who inhabited Ireland before the Firbolgs and are said to be the builders of our megalithic sites.

Newgrange: A passage tomb (chambered cairn) from the Neolithic period, around 3200 BC, older than Stonehenge and the Egyptian pyramids. Part of Brú na Bóinne (palace or mansion of the River Boyne) in County Meath, one of the world's most important prehistoric landscapes.

Ogham: ('oh-am') The first written language in Ireland, made up of groups of horizontal markings in a vertical line, writing from the bottom up. Also known as the tree language.

Oisín: ('ush-een') A character in Irish mythology who went on an immram to Tír na nÓg. When he returned, his foot accidentally touched the land of Ireland and he turned into an old, old man and died.

The Paps: (Pap: archaic English word for nipple or teat) Paps of Anu – the nipples of Anu ('an-oo'), the Mother Goddess. The Paps are two breast shaped mountains in County Kerry with a man-made cairn, like a nipple on top of each.

priestessing: bringing things, situations and people into the sacred.

rath: ('rah') Anglicised as 'rath'. A circular earthen enclosure used as a dwelling and stronghold.

Rathcroghan: ('rath-croh-han') Fort of Cruaghan, the traditional capital of Connacht and the seat of Queen Maeve in County Roscommon.

Rath Medb: ('rah maeve') Medb's enclosure at Tara, where the beanfeis took place.

Ruaidrí Ua Conchobair: ('roo-ree oh con-coo-ir') Ruaidri translates as 'red-haired king' and the modern name Rory. Ua Conchobair is O'Connor. A High King of Ireland who celebrated Bealtaine at Uisneach.

seanbhean: ('<u>shan</u>-van') An old or elder woman.

seanchai: ('<u>shan</u>-a-kee') Traditional Irish storyteller.

sean-nós: ('<u>shan</u> noess') Literally old-style. Usually refers to traditional Irish song and dance.

Scartaglen: A small village in County Kerry.

sheela-na-gigs: (From the Irish *Síle na gcíoch:* Sheila of the breasts) Ancient carved images of women displaying enlarged vulvas. Symbols of the divine feminine carved into walls of churches and castles throughout Ireland.

sidhe: ('she') The fairies or the Tuath Dé.

Sliabh Luachra: ('shleeve <u>loo</u>-a-kra') Translated as mountain of rushes. An area on the borders of Counties Kerry, Cork and Limerick, with a reputation for literature and very old, traditional music.

Solas Bhríde: ('<u>sul</u>-us <u>vree</u>-de') Brigid's Light.

St Columcille: ('<u>cullum</u>-kill') An Irish Christian saint.

The Táin: ('<u>thaw</u>-in') or *Táin Bó Cuailgne* ('<u>thaw</u>-in bow <u>koo</u>-il-nye') The Cattle Raid of Cooley. A famous story in Irish mythology, in which Queen Maeve of Connacht instigates a battle over a bull.

Teltown: From the Irish Tailtiú after the goddess and the last queen of the Firbolgs. A townland near Kells in County Meath and the burial place of Tailtiú.

Tír na nÓg: ('<u>tier</u> na <u>nogue</u>') The land of the forever young. The Valhalla of the Tuath Dé, where the souls waited to be reborn. Sometimes called Tír na mBan ('<u>tier</u> na <u>mon</u>'), the land of women.

Torc Waterfall: ('torque') A waterfall in Killarney, County Kerry.

poitín: ('<u>putch</u>-een') An illicit homemade Irish whiskey, often made with potatoes.

Uisneach: ('<u>ish</u>-nuck') A hill in County Westmeath, known in mythology as the sacred centre of Ireland. A place of assembly at Bealtaine.

ABOUT THE AUTHOR

Amantha is a mother and grandmother, celebrant, storyteller, seabhean, teacher, seer, and healer in the traditional Irish way, initiated by her grandmother.

Amantha lives in County Kerry, Ireland. She began her spiritual work publicly in 1970 as a clairvoyant before moving into trance mediumship and healing. Guided by her spirit and ancestral teachers, Amantha works with individuals and groups. She delivers apprenticeship training in Ireland, Canada and the United States on The Way of the Seabhean and Ancient Irish Shamanism. She leads sacred pilgrimages in Ireland since 1995. Her passion is the land – working through the Grandmothers, the Tuatha Dé Danann, and the Ancient Ones.

Amantha's first book is *Drinking from the Source.* Her website is **celticsouljourneys.com**

ABOUT THE SCRIBE

ORla O'Connell

M.Phil. (Creative Writing) is an Irish writer living in Strandhill, County Sligo. She was born in Tralee, County Kerry, into an Irish/English speaking household. Her novel, *The Man with No Skin*, is set in Africa and was published in 2005 by Dialogue Publishing Inc. It won first prize in fiction in the Colorado Independent Book Publisher's (CIPA) Awards and was a finalist in the (US) Independent Book Publisher's (IPPY) Awards. Her short story, *Kikuyu Grass* was shortlisted for a Hennessy Award and her stories, poems and interviews have been published in *Force 10* and other publications. Her latest novel (awaiting publication) is about the sinking of the Lusitania liner off the south coast of Ireland, in 1915.

Her website is **orlaoconnell.com**

ABOUT WOMANCRAFT

WOMANCRAFT publishing was founded on the revolutionary vision that women and words can change the world. We act as midwife to transformational women's words that have the power to challenge, inspire, heal and speak to the silenced aspects of ourselves.

We believe that:

> books are a fabulous way of transmitting powerful transformation,

> values should be juicy actions, lived out,

> ethical business is a key way to contribute to conscious change.

At the heart of our Womancraft philosophy is fairness and integrity. Creatives and women have always been underpaid. Not on our watch! We split royalties 50:50 with our authors. We work on a full circle model of giving and receiving: reaching backwards, supporting TreeSisters' reforestation projects, and forwards via Worldreader, providing books at no cost to education projects for girls and women.

We are proud that Womancraft is walking its talk and engaging so many women each year via our books and online. Join the revolution! Sign up to the mailing list at womancraftpublishing.com and find us on social media for exclusive offers:

(f) womancraftpublishing

(y) womancraftbooks

(©) womancraft_publishing

**Signed copies of all titles available from
shop.womancraftpublishing.com**

USE OF WOMANCRAFT WORK

Often women contact us asking if and how they may use our work.

We love seeing our work out in the world. We love you sharing our words further. And we ask that you respect our hard work by acknowledging the source of the words.

We are delighted for short quotes from our books – up to 200 words – to be shared as memes or in your own articles or books, provided they are clearly accompanied by the author's name and the book's title.

We are also very happy for the materials in our books to be shared amongst women's communities: to be studied by book groups, discussed in classes, read from in ceremony, quoted on social media... with the following provisos:

- If content from the book is shared in written or spoken form, the book's author and title must be referenced clearly.

- The only person fully qualified to teach the material from any of our titles is the author of the book itself. There are no accredited teachers of this work. Please do not make claims of this sort.

- If you are creating a course devoted to the content of one of our books, its title and author must be clearly acknowledged on all promotional material (posters, websites, social media posts).

- The book's cover may be used in promotional materials or social media posts. The cover art is copyright of the artist and has been licensed exclusively for this book. Any element of the book's cover or font may not be used in branding your own marketing materials when teaching the content of the book, or content very similar to the original book.

- No more than two double page spreads, or four single pages of any book may be photocopied as teaching materials.

We are delighted to offer a 20% discount of over five copies going to one address. You can order these on our webshop, or email us. If you require further clarification, email us at:

info@womancraftpublishing.com

Wild & Wise:
sacred feminine meditations for women's circles and personal awakening

Amy Bammel Wilding

The stunning debut by Amy Bammel Wilding is not merely a collection of guided meditations, but a potent tool for personal and global transformation. The meditations beckon you to explore the powerful realm of symbolism and archetypes, inviting you to access your wild and wise inner knowing.
Suitable for reflective reading or to facilitate healing and empowerment for women who gather in red tents, moon lodges, women's circles and ceremonies.

This rich resource is an answer to "what can we do to go deeper?" that many in circles want to know.

Jean Shinoda Bolen, MD

Sisters of the Solstice Moon
(Book 1 of the When She Wakes series)

Gina Martin

On the Winter Solstice, thirteen women across the world see the same terrifying vision. Their world is about to experience ravaging destruction. All that is now sacred will be destroyed. Each answers the call, to journey to Egypt, and save the wisdom of the Goddess.

An imagining… or is it a remembering… of the end of matriarchy and the emergence of global patriarchy, this book brings alive long dead cultures from around the world and brings us closer to the lost wisdoms that we know in our bones.

Moon Time:
harness the ever-changing energy of your menstrual cycle

Lucy H. Pearce

Hailed as 'life-changing' by women around the world, *Moon Time* shares a fully embodied understanding of the menstrual cycle. Full of practical insight, empowering resources, creative activities and passion, this book will put women back in touch with their body's wisdom.

This book is a wonderful journey of discovery. Lucy not only guides us through the wisdom inherent in our wombs, our cycles and our hearts, but also encourages us to share, express, celebrate and enjoy what it means to be female! A beautiful and inspiring book full of practical information and ideas.
Miranda Gray, author of *Red Moon* and *The Optimized Woman*

Medicine Woman:
reclaiming the soul of healing

Lucy H. Pearce

Nautilus Silver Award 2018

This audacious questioning of the current medical system's ability to deal with the modern epidemic of chronic illness, combines a raw personal memoir of sickness and healing, woven through with voices of dozens of other long-term sick women of the world and a feminine cultural critique that digs deep into the roots of patriarchal medicine.

Medicine Woman voices a deep yearning for a broader vision of what it means to be human than our current paradigm allows for, calling on an ancient archetype of healing, Medicine Woman, to re-vision how we can navigate sickness and harness its transformational powers in order to heal.

Packed with dozens of healing arts exercises and hundreds of medicine questions to help integrate body and mind in the healing process.

Made in the USA
Las Vegas, NV
19 March 2021